MASTER DRAWINGS

Sterling and Francine Clark as Collectors

MASTER

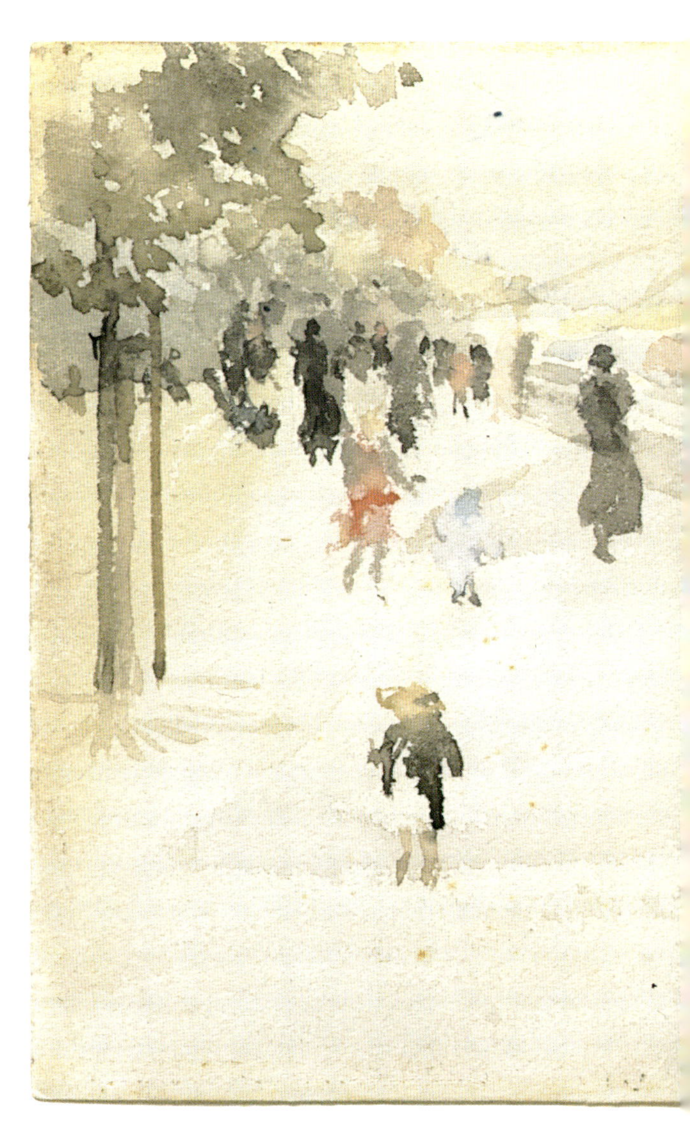

DRAWINGS

Sterling and Francine Clark
as Collectors

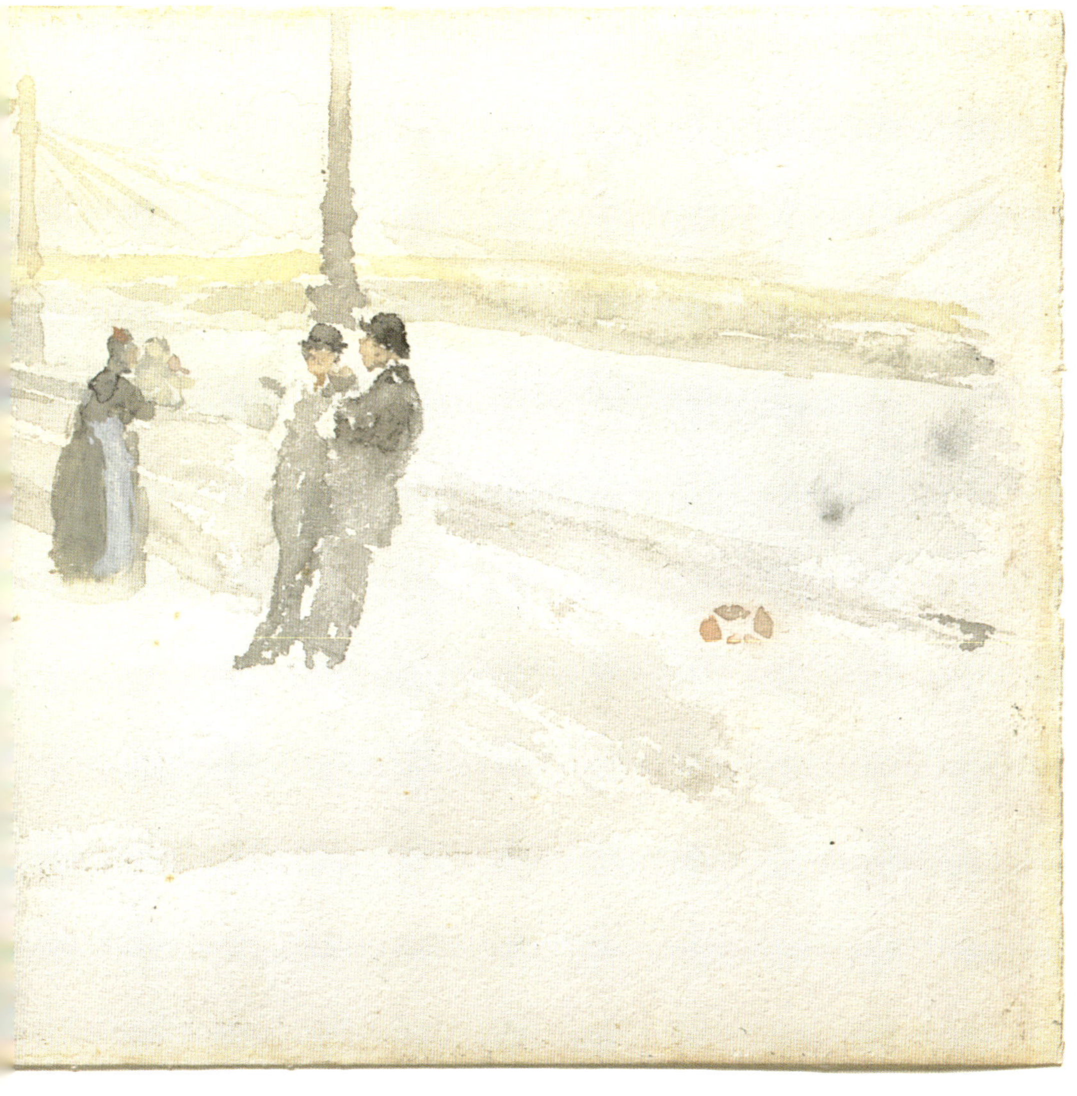

STERLING AND FRANCINE CLARK ART INSTITUTE

WILLIAMSTOWN, MASSACHUSETTS

This catalogue is published in conjunction with the exhibition *Master Drawings: Sterling and Francine Clark as Collectors* at the Sterling and Francine Clark Art Institute, Williamstown, Massachusetts, June 24–September 10, 1995.

Library of Congress Cataloging-in-Publication Data
Brooke, David S., 1931–
    Master drawings : Sterling and Francine Clark as collectors / [essay and catalogue by David S. Brooke].
       p.   cm.
     ISBN 0-931102-34-0 (pbk.)
     1. Drawing – Exhibitions. 2. Drawing – Massachusetts – Williamstown – Exhibitions. 3. Sterling and Francine Clark Art Institute – Exhibitions.
     I. Title.
NC25.W5S743 1995   95-18873
741.9'074'7441 – dc20   CIP

Editor: Elma Sanders
Designer: Jonathon Nix / Verso Design
Printer: The Studley Press
Cover: *Studies of a Flutist and Two Women*, 1712–16, Jean-Antoine Watteau (detail)
Frontispiece: *Grey and Silver: Chelsea Embankment*, c. 1887, James Abbott McNeill Whistler

CONTENTS

Foreword *by Michael Conforti* / 7
A Passion for Drawings *by David Brooke* / 9
Illustrations, Forty Master Drawings / 15
List of Artists / 40

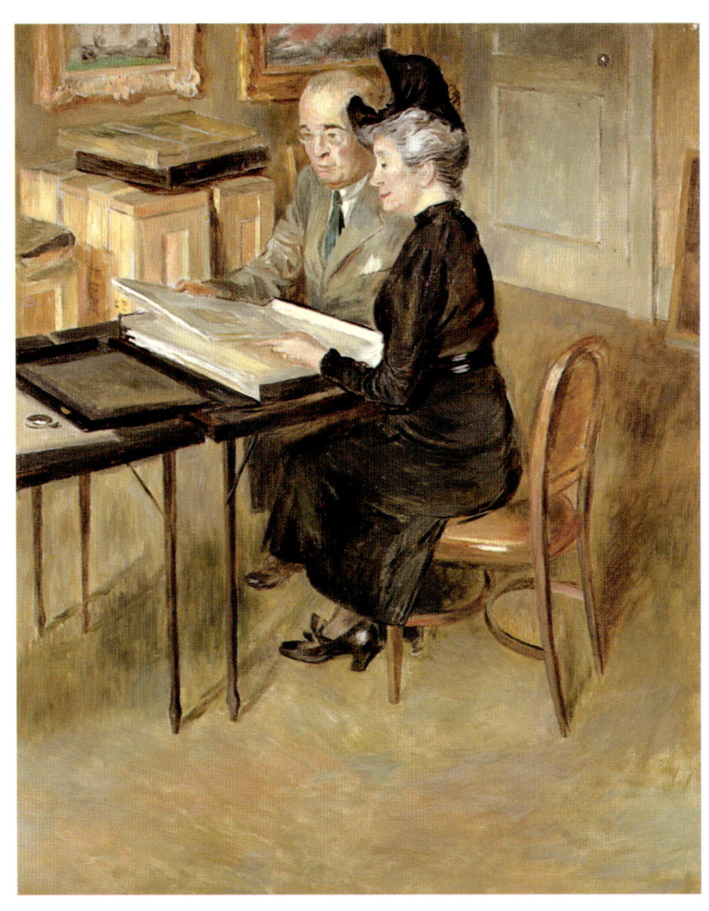

Mr. and Mrs. Clark
Paul Louis Clemens

FOREWORD

One of the finest of the collections Sterling and Francine Clark left to the Institute which they opened in 1955 is a group of old master and nineteenth-century drawings. This collection was begun in Paris in 1913 and added to over the next four decades of their lives. The quality of this group of works prompted the first catalogue of their holdings, that written by Egbert Haverkamp-Begemann and published in 1964, a catalogue now long out of print. Because the drawing collection has not been exhibited as a whole in subsequent years, we chose it for the exhibition that commemorates the fortieth anniversary of the opening of the building. David Brooke, director emeritus, agreed to write an essay and catalogue which features the finest works of Clark's original holdings. He was aided in this project by Rafael Fernandez, curator emeritus of prints and drawings, as well as by Thomas Fels, interim assistant curator in the department. Mary Jo Carpenter oversaw this publication and arranged for its design and production.

The curators of prints and drawings, from William Collins (1958–60) to, most recently, Rafael Fernandez (1975–94), have all added to Clark's initial holdings; however, the quality of Mr. and Mrs. Clark's original collection has only rarely been rivaled by recent acquisitions. It is this foundation which we continue to appreciate and which will always be remembered as the growing collection is better known and appreciated by the public.

Michael Conforti
Director

Perhaps it is wiser to examine drawings sitting down rather than standing up. They are very personal objects and ask to be perused at leisure rather than reviewed in passing like a line of soldiers. While a facsimile of a drawing is a poor substitute for the original, both at least are on paper, do not differ greatly in size, and are thus more closely related than a painting to its reproduction. So we hope that this book may give you something of the pleasure that the drawings themselves gave to the Clarks and persuade you further to explore their collection in the original. When you do, you might remember Mr. Clark's emphasis on exercising the eyes as well as the mind. When a friend asked him what she should read to better appreciate art, Clark replied,

"Look, look and look again."

David Brooke

A PASSION FOR DRAWINGS

The purpose of this book is to provide a general introduction to the Clarks' drawing collection by illustrating some of the finest examples in it. These images have been chosen from a much larger exhibition celebrating the fortieth anniversary of the Institute in 1995. While publications of the museum's Homer and Degas material appeared in 1986 and 1987, there has been no publication of the drawing collection as a whole since 1964 when the catalogue by Egbert Haverkamp-Begemann appeared. That catalogue, the first scholarly examination of any aspect of the Clarks' collection, has long been out of print.

The examples illustrated here cover a wide variety of drawing media: pencil, metal point, charcoal, ink, and watercolor, to name a few. They were made, also, for a great variety of purposes. While some were drawn as finished works of art for their own sake, others were studies for paintings, prints, and even, in one case, a stained glass window. Some were drawn from life and some from memory; others were copies after prints or paintings. Several came from distinguished collections, and a few were owned by such artists as Peter Lely, Thomas Hudson, Thomas Lawrence, and John Ruskin. Some are witnesses to interesting moments in their artists' lives. The Dürer records a visit to the Brussels Zoological Gardens in 1521; the Toulouse-Lautrec circus drawing is one of a series made while he was a patient in a sanitarium at Neuilly in 1899.

Including the pastels and watercolors, nearly four hundred drawings were acquired by Robert Sterling Clark and Francine Clark over a period of some forty years. The collection seems to have been assembled largely for personal pleasure, without any master plan or desire to create a historical survey. In general it follows the same outlines as does the painting collection, with relatively few older masters and a particular focus on the nineteenth century and on France. It is also marked by "sub-collections" of favorite artists, and there are a considerable number of anecdotal and illustrative drawings which were collected for the appeal of the subject matter rather than for their quality or importance. The Clarks apparently did not rely on advisors, and a vigorous note of independence sounds throughout Mr. Clark's diaries and letters. Dealers, on the other hand, may well have played a significant role. "I never saw a museum man who knew much," said Mr. Clark to a friend who proposed showing a Turner watercolor to someone at The Metropolitan Museum of Art for expertise; he recommended instead his favorite firm of Knoedler's. When someone congratulated him on having a "natural eye," Clark replied that while part of it might be natural, the rest had been educat-

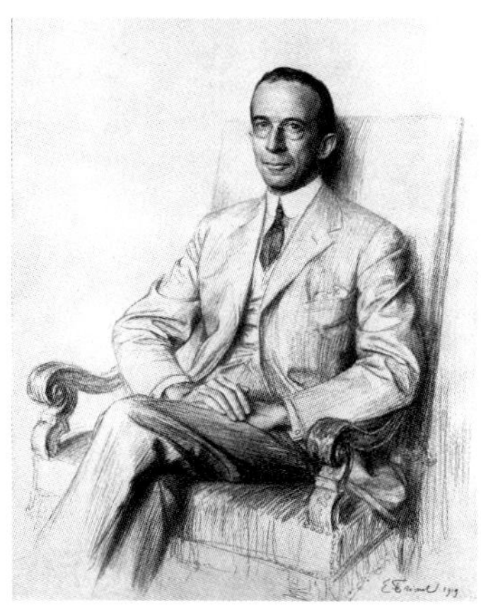

ed by Maurice Hamman, who was with the Paris branch of the firm. His personal relationship with the London firm of Colnaghi's, from which he bought many of his best drawings (and paintings) between 1913 and 1921, remains uncharted, though he clearly respected Gustavus Mayer, who joined that firm shortly before Clark started collecting.

Robert Sterling Clark was raised amidst the art collection of his father, Alfred Corning Clark. This included a number of American drawings, among them several by Blum and the Whistler *Grey and Silver* illustrated here. Robert did not become a serious collector, however, until his mid-thirties. Prior to this, he had led a rather adventurous life, including service in the army from 1899 to 1905 and an expedition to northern China in 1908 and 1909. He then inherited a considerable fortune – and some paintings – from his mother and in 1911 settled down with great relish to the life of a collector in Paris, making numerous trips to London where he acquired many of his paintings and, beginning in 1913, old master drawings from the firm of Colnaghi's. At about the same time he met Francine Clary, who had been a member of the Comédie-Française from 1904 to 1910. They were married in 1919 – coincidentally, a peak year in their collecting of drawings – and there are two pencil portraits of them by Emile Friant done at this time (reproduced here and on facing page). Francine shared her husband's passion for collecting, and he in turn had considerable respect for her judgment. Mr. Clark called her his "touchstone in judging pictures" and an "excellent judge, much better than I am at times."

From the few letters that survive from this period, it is evident that Clark found these early years in Paris an intoxicating experience. He wrote to his family and friends in the States about the thrills of book collecting, of visits to art dealers, of training horses, and even of planning a second expedition to China. "You will not believe it," he wrote to a friend, "but according to the best authorities, horsemanship is an art just like fiddling Beethoven, singing Pagliacci, cooking like Savarin or painting pictures like Ruysdael."

He seems to have brought the same zest to his collecting of drawings, which was impressively launched in 1913 with the purchase of a fine miniature of St. Mark by Bourdichon, Rembrandt's *Christ Finding the Apostles Asleep*, and the first of two landscapes by Gainsborough. The serious collecting of drawings was a relatively new practice in the United States. In the nineteenth century, American collectors of drawings had been few and far between (James Bowdoin, James Jackson Jarves, and John Witt Randall come especially to mind), and it was only in the early twentieth century that drawings began to be more widely appreciated as works of art and not as historical documents alone. The activities of John Pierpont Morgan and Paul Sachs in the early years of the century helped to create a favorable environment for such distinguished col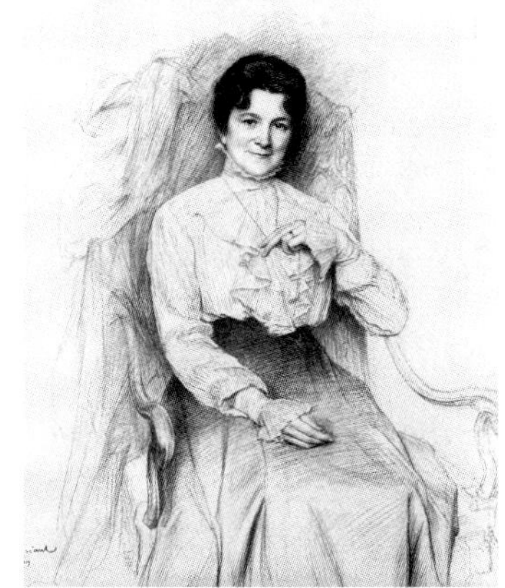lectors as Lessing Rosenwald and Grenville Winthrop. Clark must be considered as one of this group who first brought to America, and ultimately to its museums, some of the finest old master drawings then on the market.

By 1918 Clark had already assembled some of his best examples, which included an eclectic variety of high-quality drawings by Perugino, Rembrandt, Gainsborough, Delacroix, Corot, and Manet, among others. The year 1919 was to be a peak year for acquisitions, with works by Dürer, Rembrandt, Rubens, Watteau, Toulouse-Lautrec, and Degas entering the collection. Clark bought no fewer than seventeen drawings at the fourth auction of Degas's estate in July 1919. He wrote much later to a friend: "I well remember the Degas sale after the First World War. I bought a few things like the portrait and some drawings: my only regret is that I did not buy more." A remarkable group of drawings by the two Tiepolos was to follow in 1920 and 1921.

Clark was also very interested in what he called "the illustrators of the last century" – principally Jean-Louis Forain, Constantin Guys, and Jules Chéret – buying a considerable number of their drawings and watercolors. He made a clear distinction in aesthetic values between some of these works and his master drawings. In 1916 he wrote to his brother Stephen about a visit he made to an art publisher: "I think I must have gone over close to a thousand drawings of all sorts, shapes and sizes. I learned the names of a lot of men I did not know anything about and got a lot of practice for the modest sum of 800 francs which I paid for six drawings. They are not great works of art – I did not expect that – but they are nice drawings illustrative of our times."

In 1915, Clark had something of a field day purchasing the work of Forain and Chéret. He had met the latter and described his posters as "very charming, very light and extremely Parisian. They are sort of 18th century things in the 20th, very much influenced by Watteau and Fragonard." It should be noted that the last two artists were much appreciated by Clark and often mentioned in his diaries. He purchased three drawings by Watteau and a drawing and a painting (now given to a follower) by Fragonard.

The paintings and drawings which Clark bought with such enthusiasm between 1912 and 1922 when he was in Paris clearly outlined the future shape of these areas of the Clark collection. The earlier Italian and Flemish sections were well established by 1922 and only occasionally added to thereafter. The eighteenth-century acquisitions, on the other hand, continued more consistently through the following two decades. And though the dominant nineteenth-century section was to be greatly enlarged during the next thirty years, its principal outlines had been laid down before 1922, when works by several of Clark's favorites – Sargent, Homer, Corot, Degas, and Renoir – had already been acquired. Only Monet, Pissarro, and Sisley were not yet represented, and they would follow in the 1930s.

In the earlier years of Clark's collecting there are some instances in which drawings and paintings by the same artists were bought about the same time: Gainsborough, G. B. Tiepolo, Homer, and Puvis de Chavannes, for example. While it is difficult to point to any overall plan for the collections of drawings and paintings, one wonders whether some drawings – by Rubens and Watteau, for example – were selected both for their quality and as worthy substitutes for paintings by those masters, which could not easily be found or afforded. The two collections dovetail in a remarkable way, the drawings often seeming to complement rather than echo the paintings.

While the Clarks' major drawing acquisitions in the 1920s and 1930s were fewer, several excellent examples entered the collection during this period. Among these were the Rubens wash of Thomas Howard, the Watteau chalk *Studies of a Flutist and Two Women,* and Morisot's watercolor of a harbor scene. Acquisitions of watercolors by Homer and drawings by Degas (two of the artists he most admired) also continued. It was in this period between the wars, following a focus on impressionist paintings in the mid-1930s, that the Clarks bought the Cassatt pastel *Child with Red Hat*, a Monet charcoal of Rouen, and three circus drawings by Toulouse-Lautrec. The last were chosen by Mrs. Clark, as Mr. Clark noted in his diary: "[The dealer] produced six excellent colored drawings of scenes at the circus – they were so good I phoned Francine.... She chose the three I thought she would like and I bought them."

Mr. Clark had another period of energetic acquisition between 1935 and 1943, though many of the drawings he bought were from his "illustrators" and generally of less importance. In the early 1940s he purchased the splendid Fragonard *Les Jets d'eau* (*The Fountains*), about which he had a characteristic wrangle with Felix Wildenstein. He wrote: "I pointed to the *Jets d'eau* and said, 'I'll give you $12,000 for that one.' It took Felix off his feet. 'Make an effort Mr. Clark' (he exclaimed). He did not refuse the $12,000 but proposed $14,000. I said 'No, think of $13,000.'" The drawing was finally acquired for $12,000. In 1939, Clark had written that he "gave Felix Wildenstein a lecture: I expect to be given the lowest prices which are fair both to me and to you. I do not bargain and pay quickly as you well know from my reputation."

Prud'hon's *La Source* (*The Spring*) (which much impressed Mrs. Clark with its "wonderful sculptural quality"), Turner's luminescent watercolor of Brunnen, and Whistler's black chalk study for *Weary* also entered the collection at this time. As with his painting acquisitions in the 1940s and early 1950s, these can be seen as a strong finish to Mr. Clark's collecting career. It is rather touching to note that one of his last purchases, in 1953, was *Aimons-Nous* (*Let's Make Love*), a lively and colorful gouache for a poster by his old favorite Chéret. A few years earlier he had hung four of Chéret's posters in his country house in Upperville, Virginia, noting briefly but enthusiastically, "effect delightful and such lovely coloring."

In the late 1930s and early 1940s Clark had begun to look back over his entire collection and consider an appropriate home for it. At one time he kept many of his drawings at Knoedler's, and in 1939, shortly before the outbreak of the Second World War, he noted in his diary: "Walked to Knoedler's 57th St. – Print Department. Checked over the numerous boxes of my drawings. Really a good lot. Collins and Harrington astonished at the Daumiers and Tiepolos."

At some point, he seems to have transferred his collection, or part of it, to Durand-Ruel's, which stood next to Knoedler's on what Clark referred to as "the 57th Street Art Island," a paradise which he often visited. Clark was personally friendly with Charles Durand-Ruel and acquired from the firm many of his Renoirs and also a few drawings, among them the Degas *Violinist*. A double portrait of the Clarks by their young friend Paul Clemens (reproduced on page 6) shows them at Durand-Ruel's in 1942 looking through a solander box. Clark had earlier taken Clemens and his wife and others to look at his drawing collection there. "I took them all upstairs," he wrote, "and showed them some of my fine drawings. Daumier, Tiepolo, Winslow Homer, Rubens, etc. I had an appreciative audience, I think!!"

The Clarks' collection of drawings – as that of paintings – was clearly a labor of love. They collected what they liked personally, freely indulging themselves in their favorites. Mr. Clark obviously admired traditional draftsmanship. When he came across the early Degas drawing of a bearded man (which was "greatly admired" by Mrs. Clark) at Durand-Ruel's in 1938, he noted that it was "a magnificent drawing, as fine as a da Vinci or Holbein."

Mr. Clark's enthusiasm for works of art and his enjoyment of conversations with the dealers about the market come through clearly in his letters and diaries. The dealers, in turn, seem to have found him a congenial, if somewhat eccentric and outspoken, customer. While he was a man of strong opinions, he enjoyed keeping the "boys" (as he called them) guessing as to exactly what picture might tempt him. He seems to have bought as the occasion arose, often on impulse, and would sometimes turn down something which he admired but considered overpriced on the current market. The first curator of prints and drawings at the Institute, appointed after Clark's death in 1956, was his old friend William Collins from Knoedler's. Clark had once jocularly described himself to Collins as "the oddest customer you have." After a pause, Collins had replied, "No, I would not say that. You have a great eye but I do say you are an unpredictable buyer." Clark was much amused at the remark and said, "That is a great compliment, to my way of thinking. . . . I had a lot of fun buying."

FORTY MASTER DRAWINGS

NOTES TO THE CAPTIONS

Measurements give height before width.

The medium of support is paper unless otherwise noted.

The number on the last line of each caption is the accession number assigned by the Clark Art Institute and is the unique identification for that drawing.

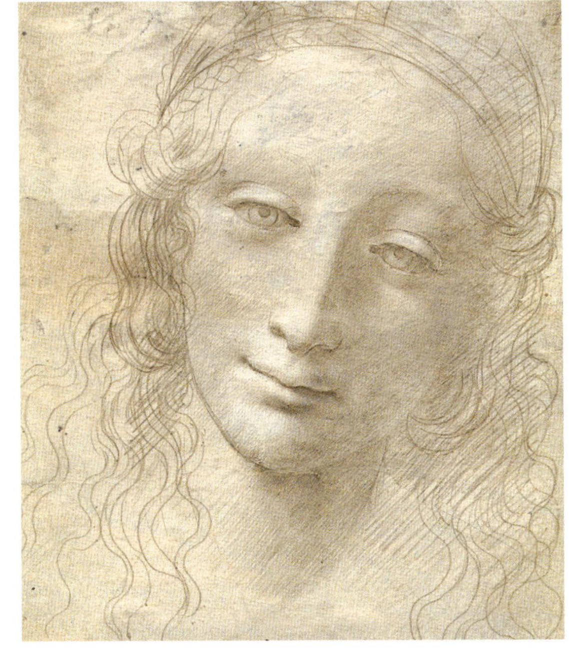

ATTRIBUTED TO GIOVANNI BOLTRAFFIO

Italian (Milanese), 1467–1516

Head of a Woman

Date unknown

Metal point

$5\frac{7}{8}$ x $4\frac{7}{8}$ in. (15.0 x 12.4 cm)

Inscribed lower left: *Leonardo da vinci*

Acquired 1917 (Colnaghi, London)

1955.1470

JEAN BOURDICHON

French, c. 1457–1521

Saint Mark

c. 1510

Tempera on parchment

$7\frac{11}{16}$ x $5\frac{11}{16}$ in. (19.5 x 14.5 cm)

Unsigned

Acquired 1913 (Bonjean, Paris)

1955.1873

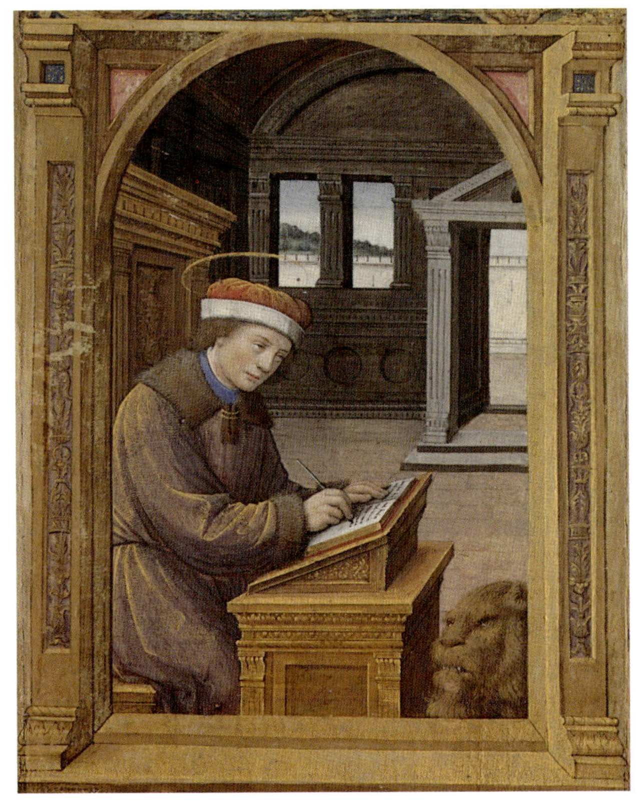

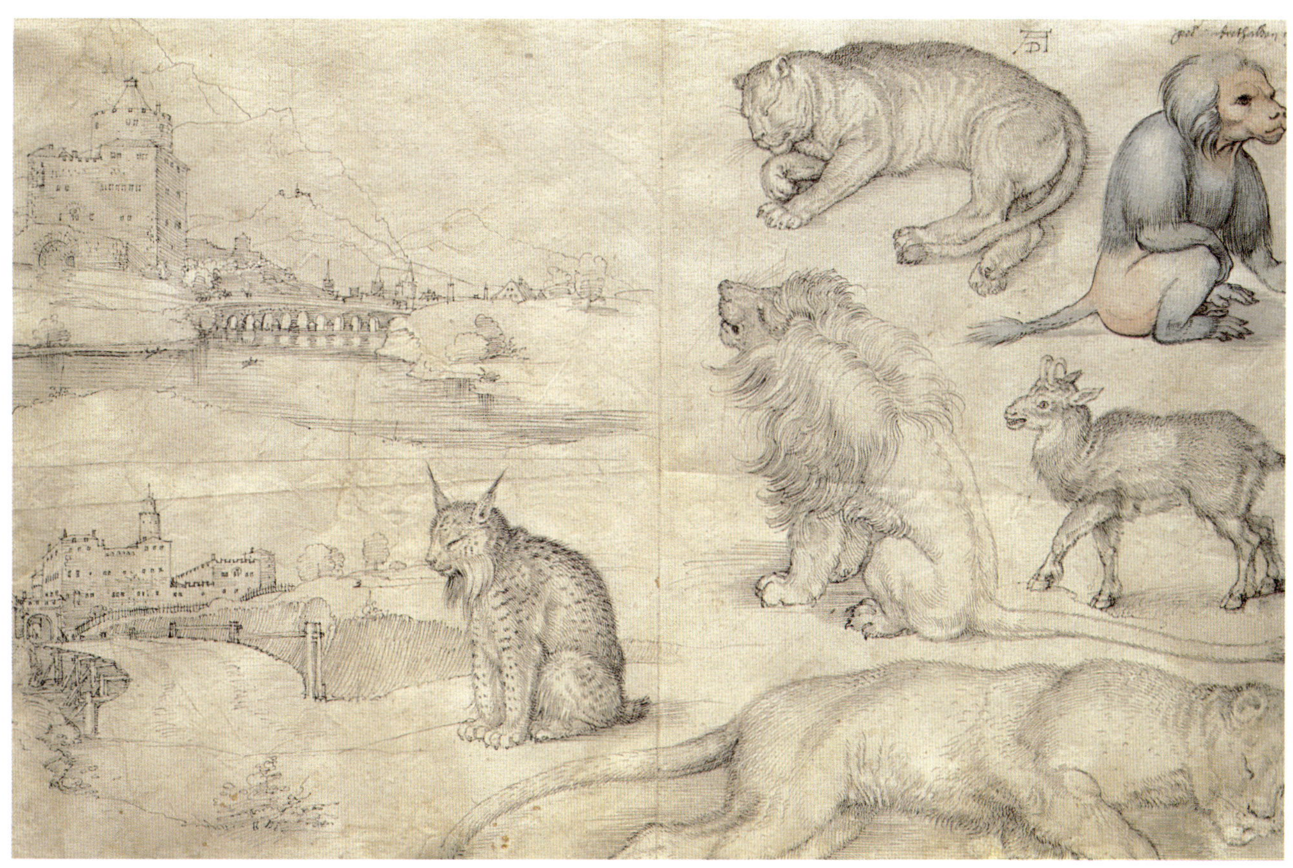

Albrecht Dürer

German, 1471–1528
Sketches of Animals and Landscapes
1521
Ink and wash
10⁷⁄₁₆ x 15⅝ in. (26.4 x 39.7 cm)
Signed with monogram and dated upper right: *1521*
Acquired 1919 (Colnaghi, London)
1955.1848

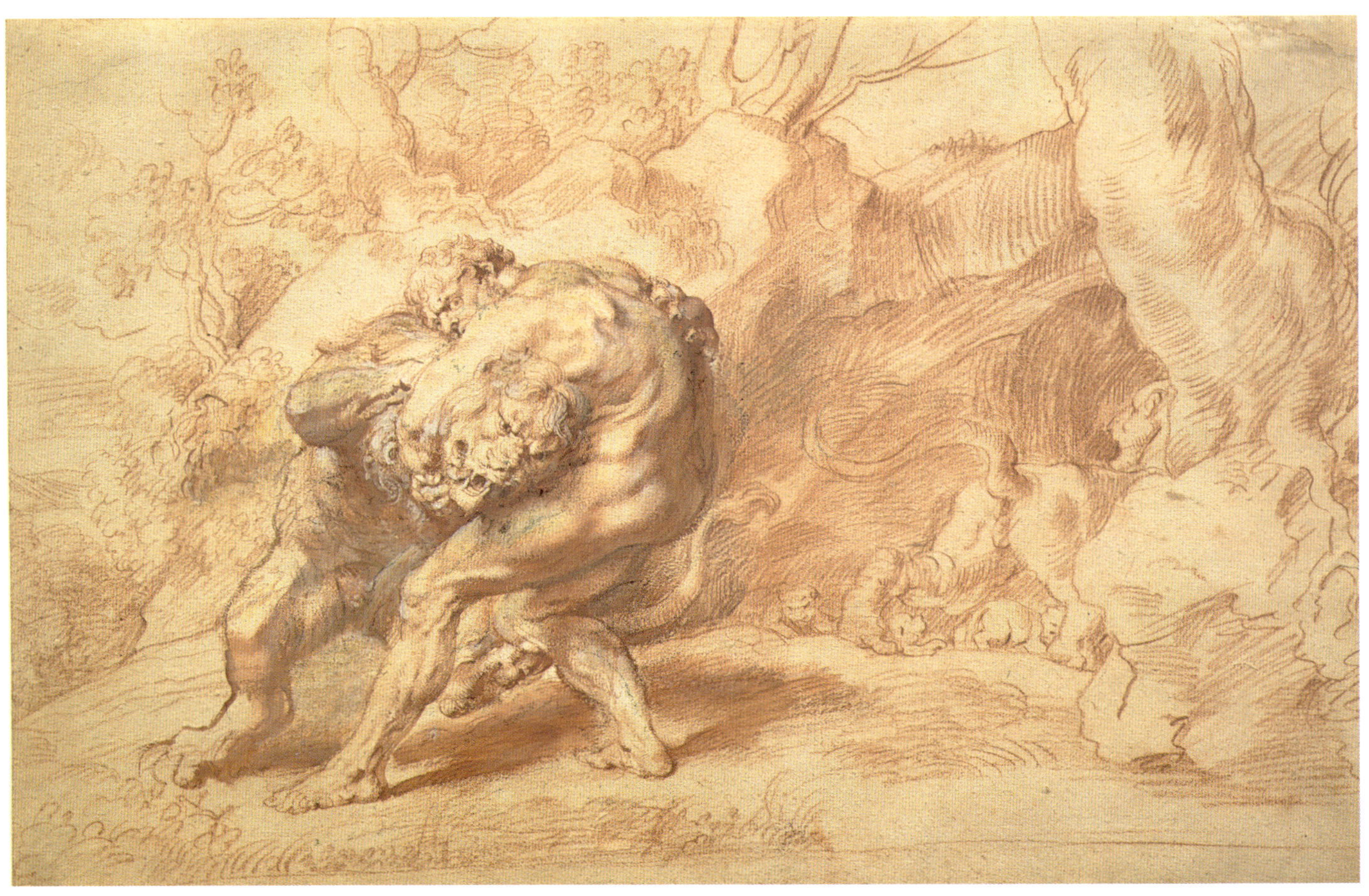

PETER PAUL RUBENS

Flemish, 1577–1640
Hercules Strangling the Nemean Lion
c. 1620
Chalk, ink, and gouache
12½ x 19 1/16 in. (31.8 x 48.4 cm)
Unsigned
Acquired 1919 (Colnaghi, London)
1955.992

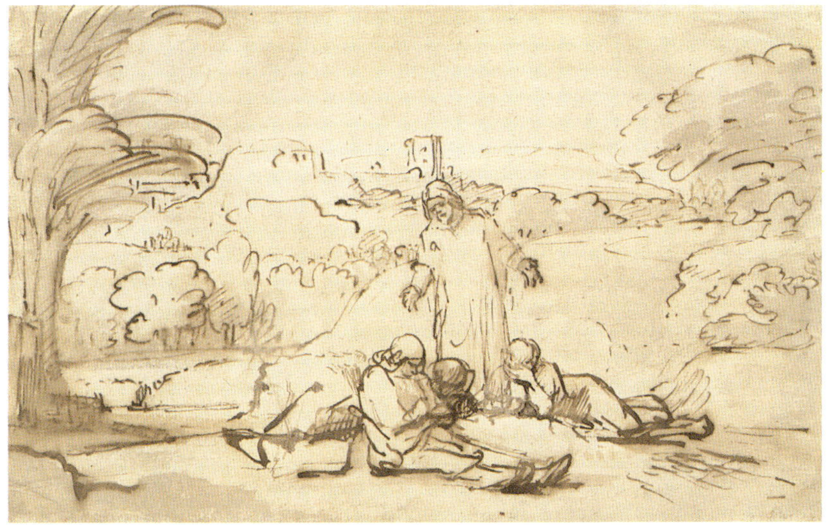

REMBRANDT HARMENSZ. VAN RIJN

Dutch, 1606–1669
Christ Finding the Apostles Asleep
c. 1654
Ink and wash
7¼ x 11 in. (18.3 x 28.0 cm)
Unsigned
Acquired 1913 (Colnaghi, London)
1955.994

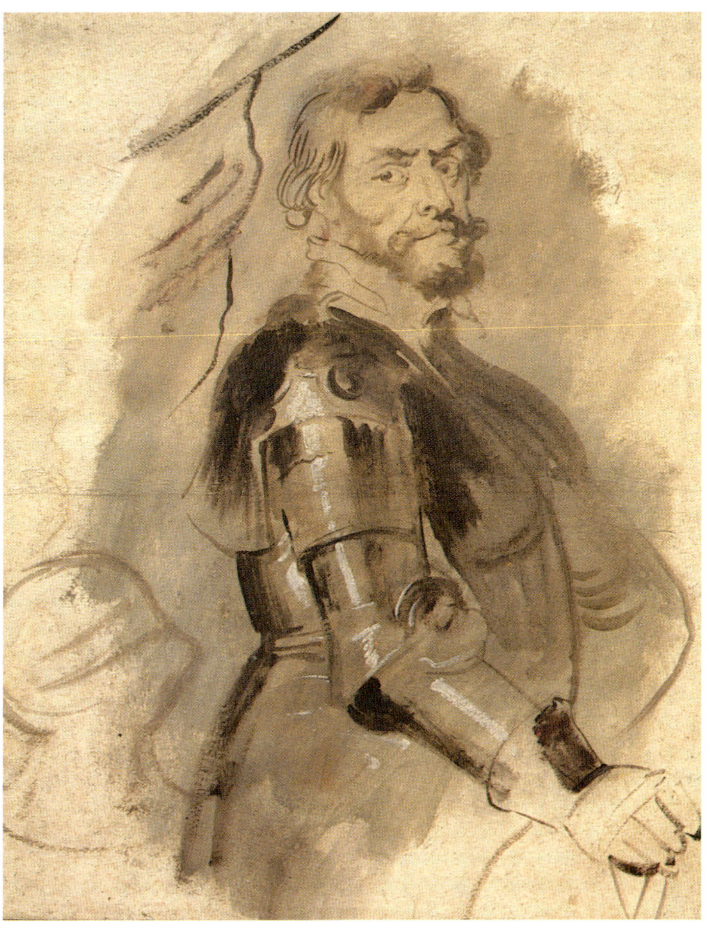

PETER PAUL RUBENS

Flemish, 1577–1640
Portrait of Thomas Howard, Earl of Arundel
1629–30
Ink, oil, and wash
18¼ x 14 in. (46.3 x 36.5 cm)
Unsigned
Acquisition date unknown
1955.991

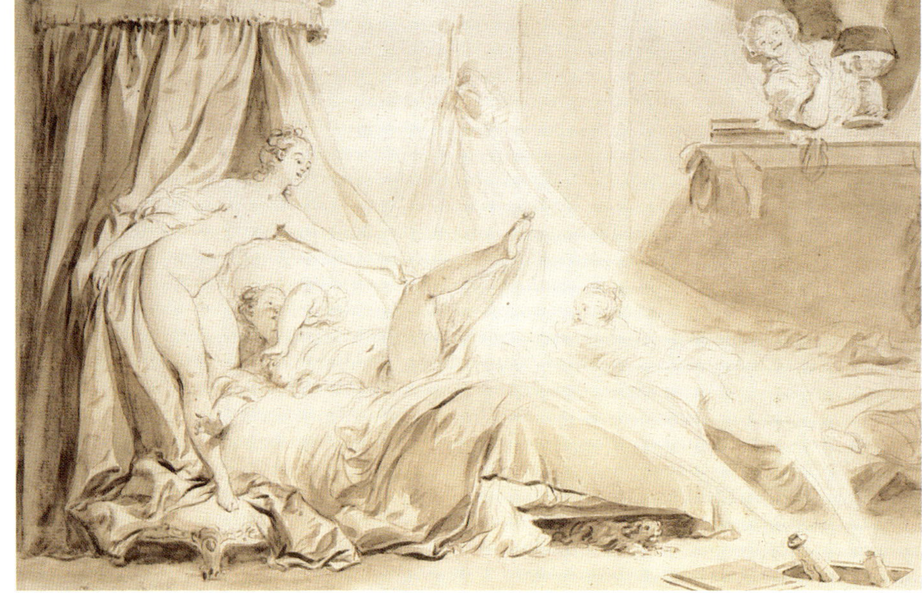

JEAN-HONORÉ FRAGONARD

French, 1732–1806
Les Jets d'eau (*The Fountains*)
c. 1767
Ink, wash, and pencil
10 $\frac{7}{16}$ x 15 $\frac{1}{8}$ in. (26.5 x 38.4 cm)
Unsigned
Acquired 1941 (Wildenstein,
New York)
1955.1967

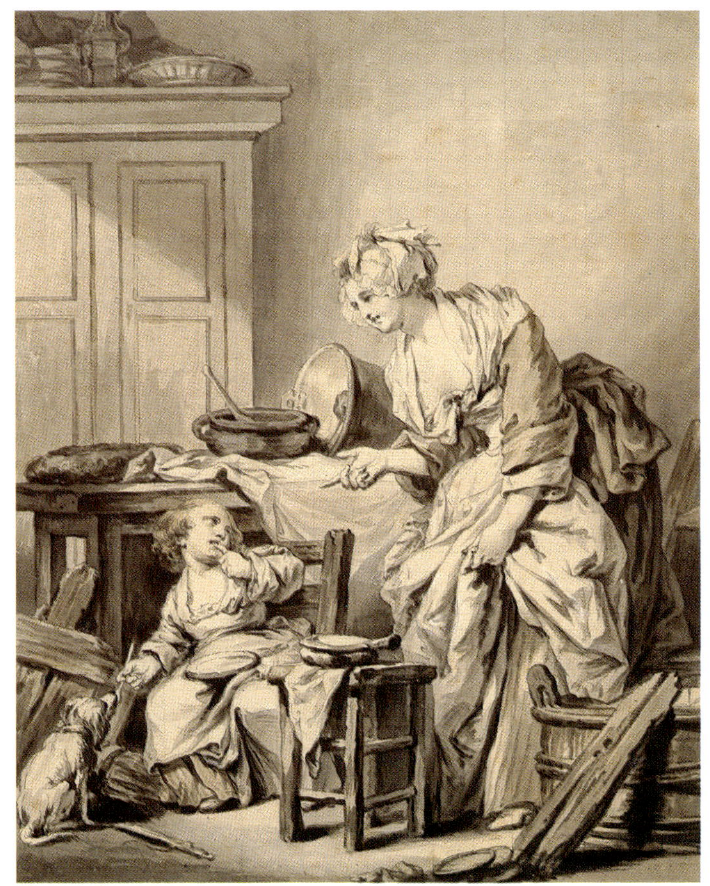

JEAN-BAPTISTE GREUZE

French, 1725–1805
The Motherly Reprimand
c. 1765
Ink and wash
18 x 13 $\frac{1}{2}$ in. (45.6 x 34.4 cm)
Signed lower left: *J. B. Greuze*
Acquired 1936 (d'Heucqueville
sale, Paris)
1955.1660

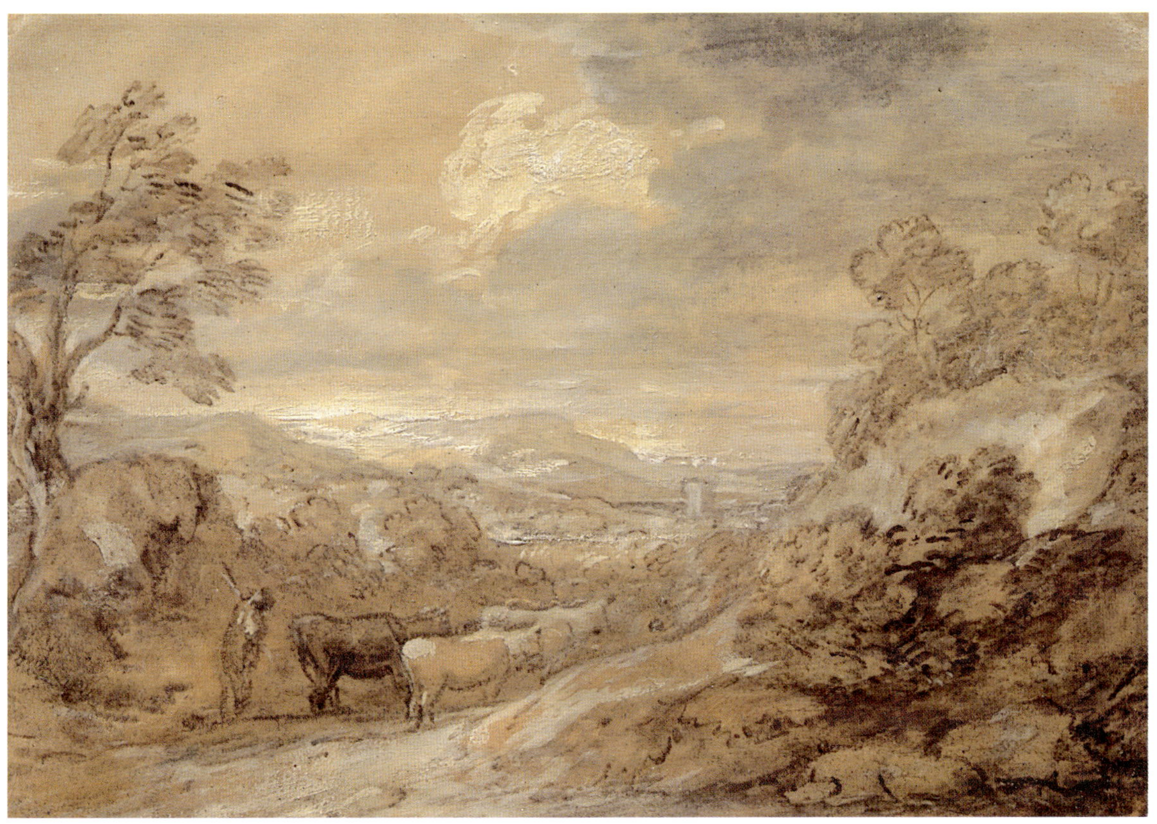

Thomas Gainsborough

British, 1727–1788
Herdsman and Cattle
1770–80
Chalk, watercolor, and oil
8⅞ x 12¼ in. (22.5 x 31.0 cm)
Unsigned
Acquired 1918 (Colnaghi, London)
1955.1971

PIERRE PAUL PRUD'HON
French, 1758–1823
La Source (*The Spring*)
c. 1801
Chalk
21$\frac{3}{16}$ x 15$\frac{5}{16}$ in. (53.8 x 38.9 cm)
Unsigned
Acquired 1940 (Seligman,
New York)
1955.833

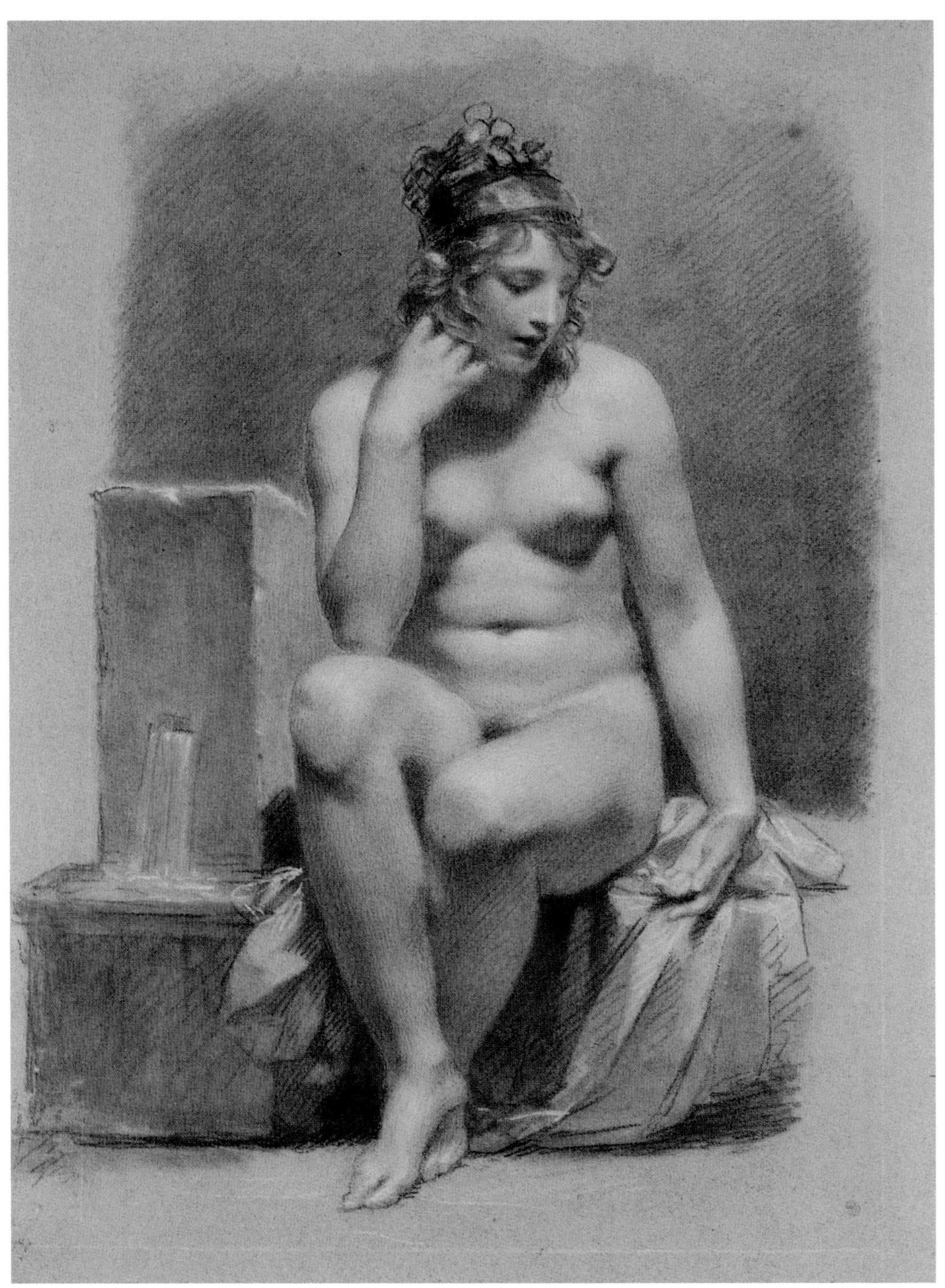

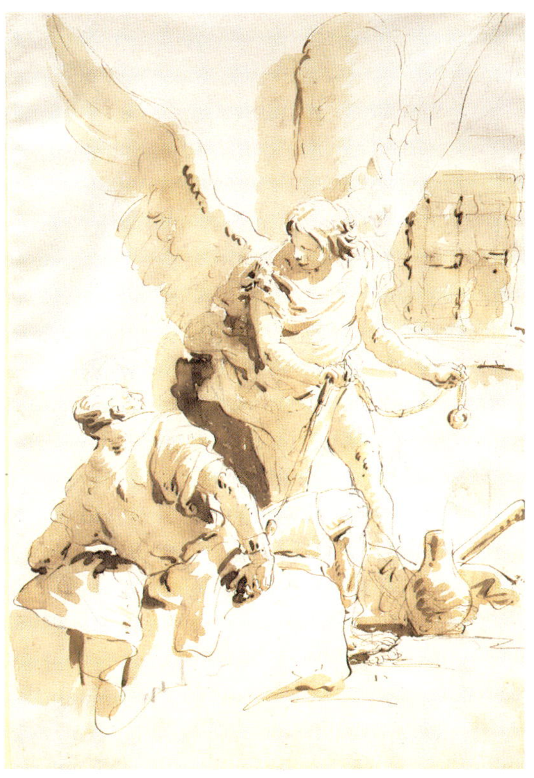

GIOVANNI BATTISTA TIEPOLO

Italian, 1696–1770
The Liberation of Saint Peter
1725–35
Ink and wash over chalk
17⅛ x 11⁷⁄₁₆ in. (43.4 x 29.0 cm)
Unsigned
Acquired 1920 (Knoedler, Paris)
1955.1465

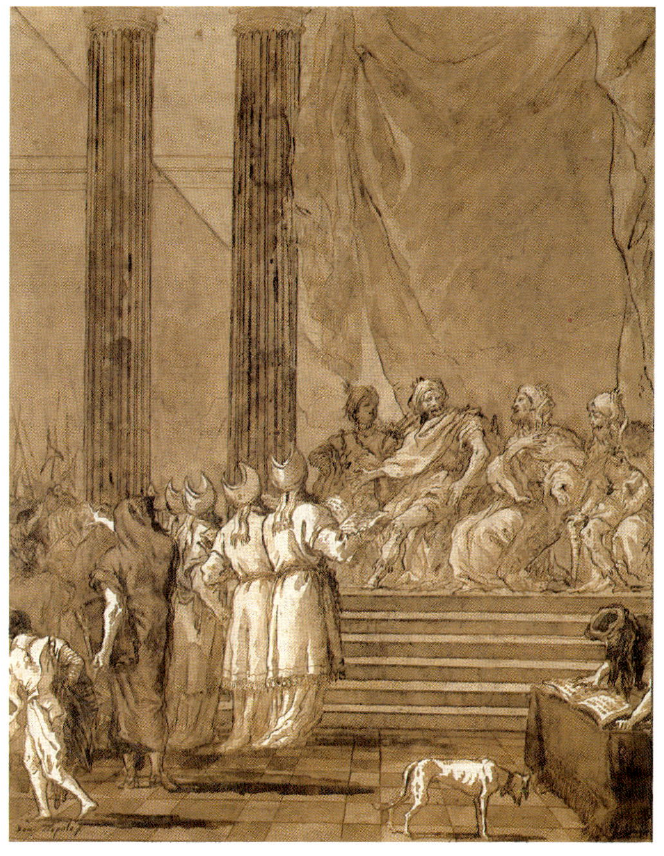

GIOVANNI DOMENICO TIEPOLO

Italian, 1727–1804
A Disputation between Kings and Priests
1770–90
Ink and wash over chalk
19⅜ x 15¹⁄₁₆ in. (49.1 x 38.2 cm)
Signed lower left: *Dom. Tiepolo f*
Acquired 1921 (Knoedler, Paris)
1955.1460

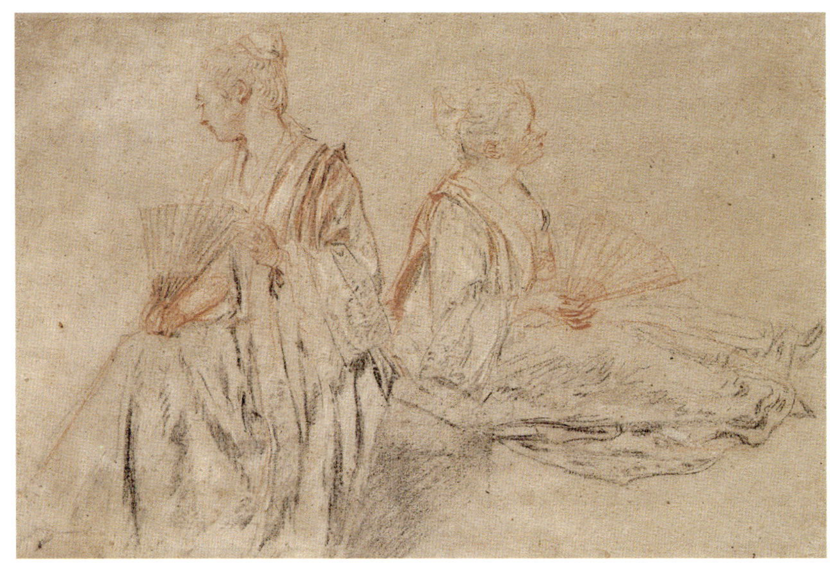

JEAN-ANTOINE WATTEAU

French, 1684–1721
Two Studies of a Woman with a Fan
before 1716
Chalk
9¾ x 13¹⁵⁄₁₆ in. (24.8 x 35.4) cm
Unsigned
Acquired 1921 (Colnaghi, London)
1955.1852

JEAN-ANTOINE WATTEAU

French, 1684–1721
Studies of a Flutist and Two Women
1712–16
Chalk
10½ x 9¹⁄₁₆ in. (26.6 x 23.1 cm)
Unsigned
Acquired 1935 (Knoedler, New York)
1955.1839

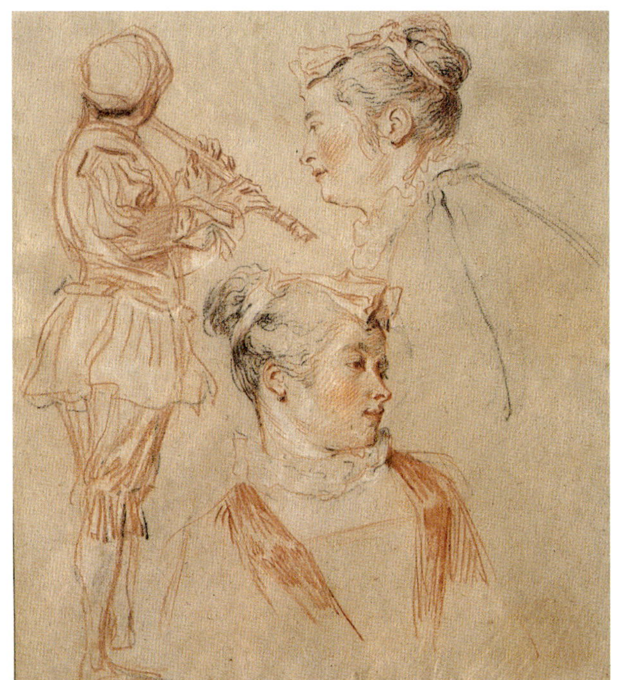

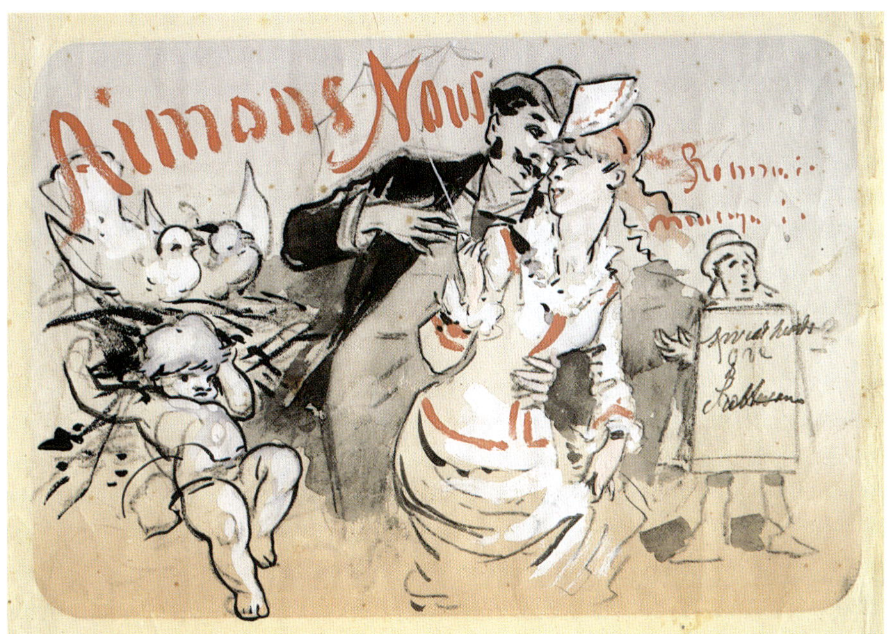

JULES CHÉRET

French, 1836–1932
Aimons-Nous (*Let's Make Love*)
1870–80
Ink, wash, and gouache over chalk
11¼ x 14⅝ in. (28.6 x 37.1 cm)
Inscribed: *Aimons Nous/*[illegible]
Acquired 1953 (Knoedler, New York)
1955.1534

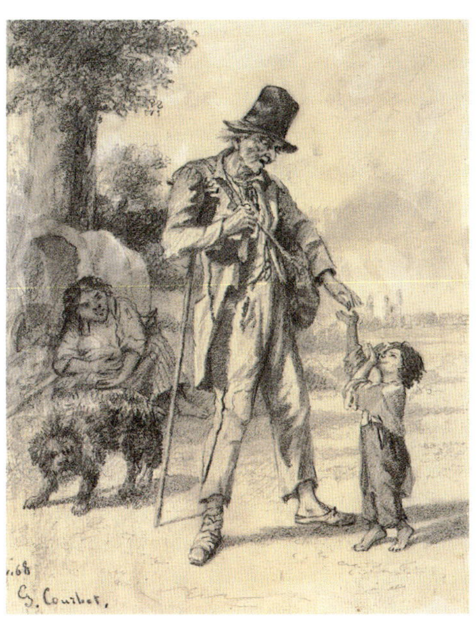

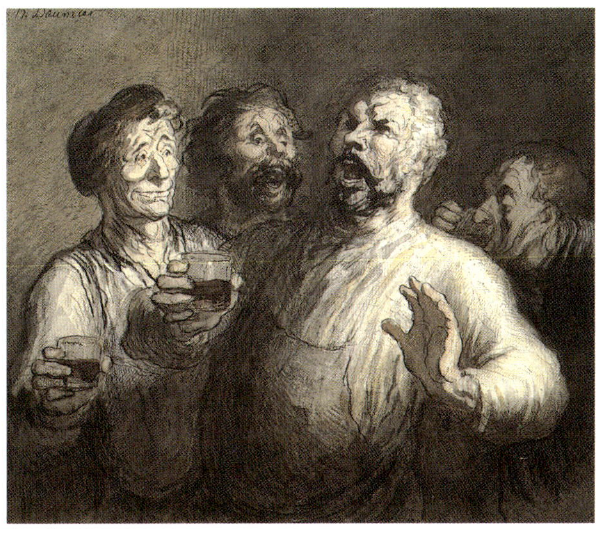

GUSTAVE COURBET

French, 1819–1877
Alms from a Beggar, at Ornans
1868
Pencil
11¼ x 8¹³⁄₁₆ in. (28.5 x 22.4 cm)
Signed and dated lower left: *68/G. Courbet*
Acquired 1943 (Knoedler, New York)
1955.1846

HONORÉ DAUMIER

French, 1808–1879
The Song
c. 1859
Chalk, ink, wash, and watercolor
9⁵⁄₁₆ x 10⁷⁄₁₆ in. (23.7 x 26.6 cm)
Signed upper left: *h. Daumier*
Acquisition date unknown
1955.1504

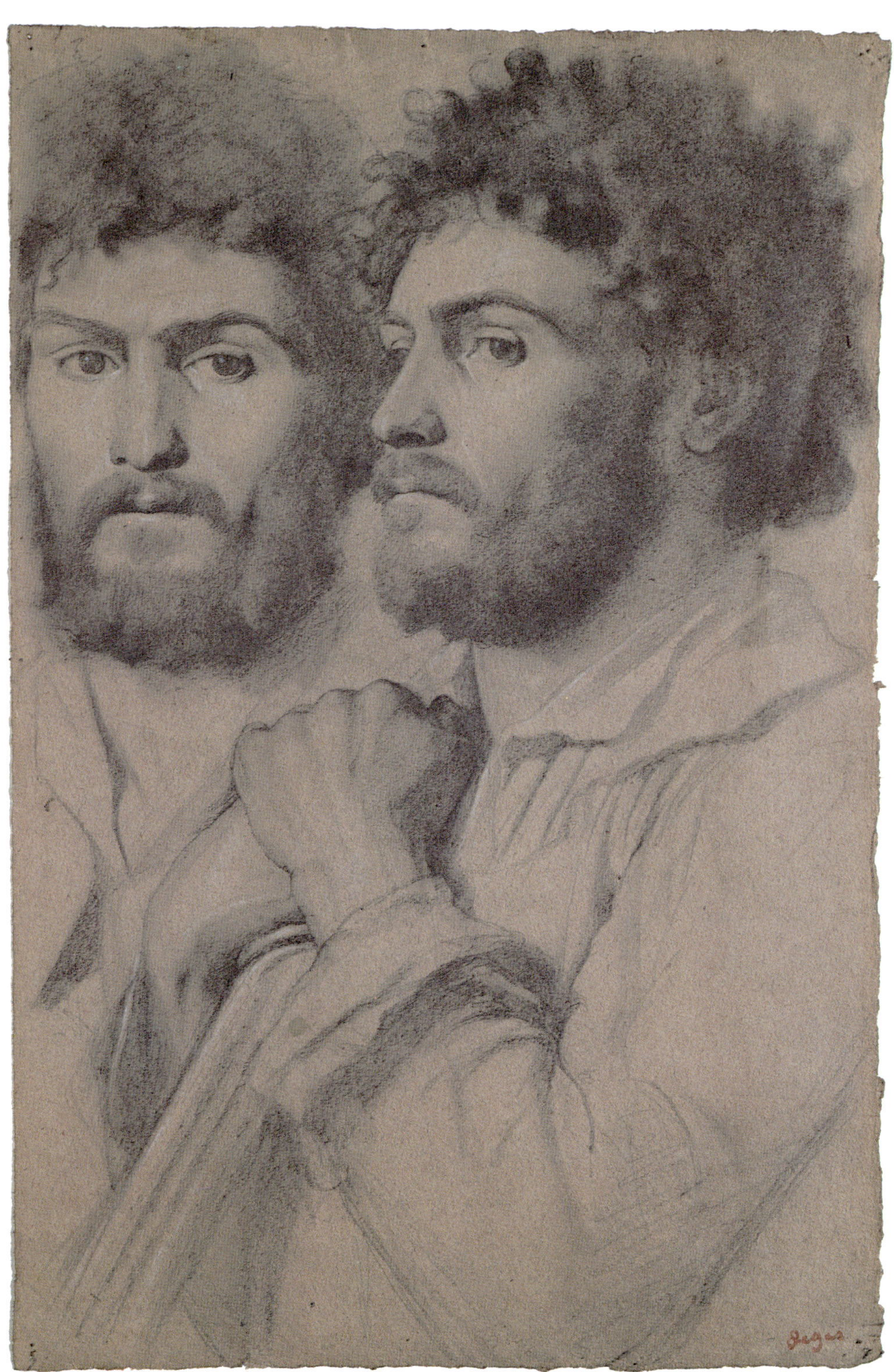

Hilaire Germain
Edgar Degas

French, 1834–1917
Two Portrait Studies of a Man
c. 1856
Pencil
17⅝ x 11¼ in. (44.8 x 28.6 cm)
Stamped lower right: *degas*
Acquired 1939 (Durand-Ruel,
New York)
1955.1393

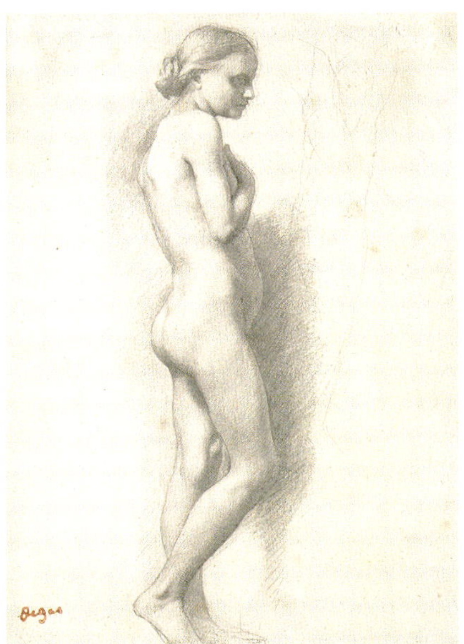

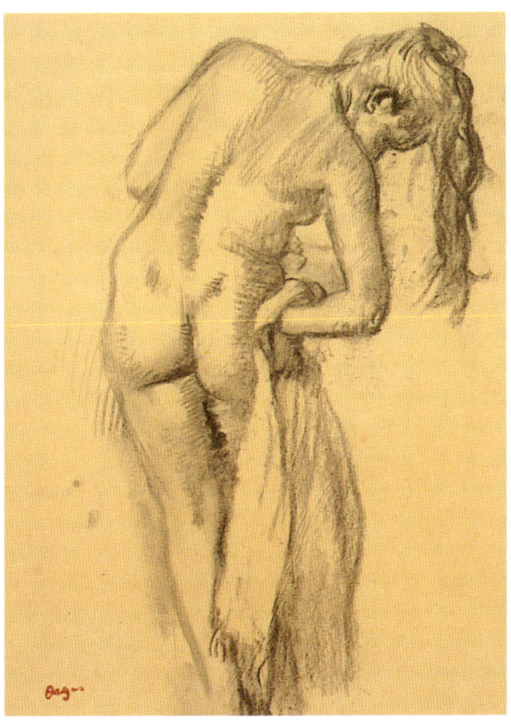

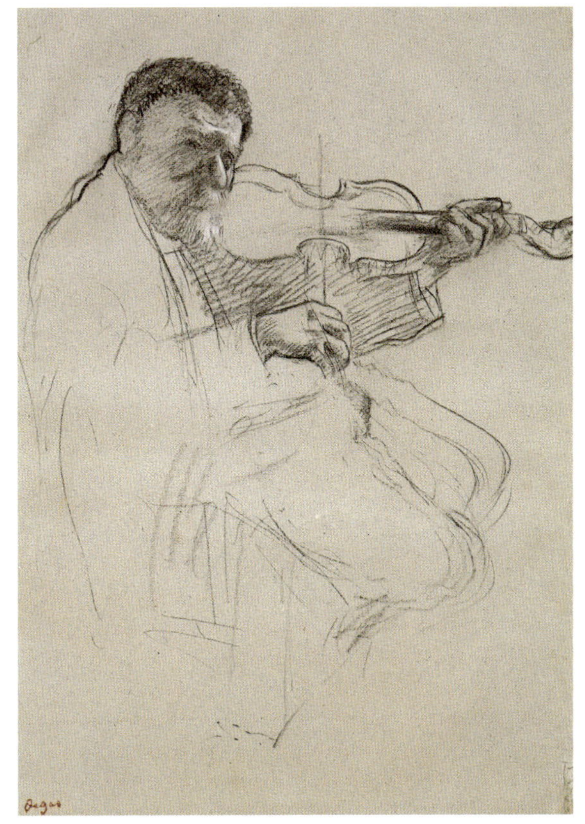

HILAIRE GERMAIN EDGAR
DEGAS

French, 1834–1917
Standing Nude
c. 1863
Pencil
11½ x 8⁹⁄₁₆ in. (29.1 x 21.8 cm)
Unsigned
Acquired 1919 (Georges Petit sale,
Paris)
1955.1847

HILAIRE GERMAIN EDGAR
DEGAS

French, 1834–1917
The Violinist
c. 1878
Charcoal
17⅛ x 12⅛ in. (43.5 x 30.9 cm)
Unsigned
Acquired 1938 (Durand-Ruel, Paris)
1955.1395

HILAIRE GERMAIN EDGAR
DEGAS

French, 1834–1917
After the Bath
c. 1891
Charcoal
13⅞ x 10 in. (35.2 x 25.4 cm)
Stamped lower left: *degas*
Acquired 1919 (Georges Petit sale,
Paris)
1955.1408

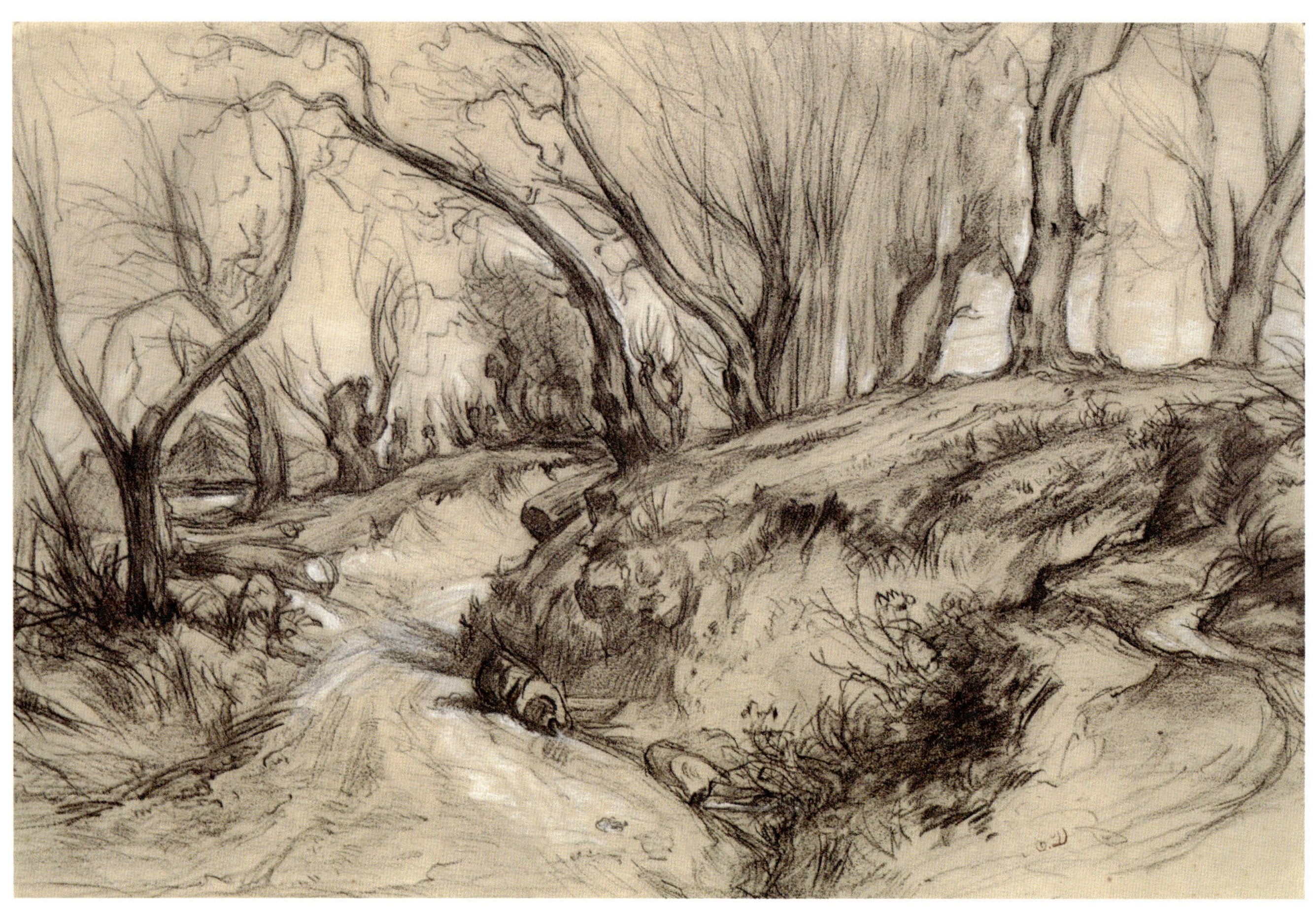

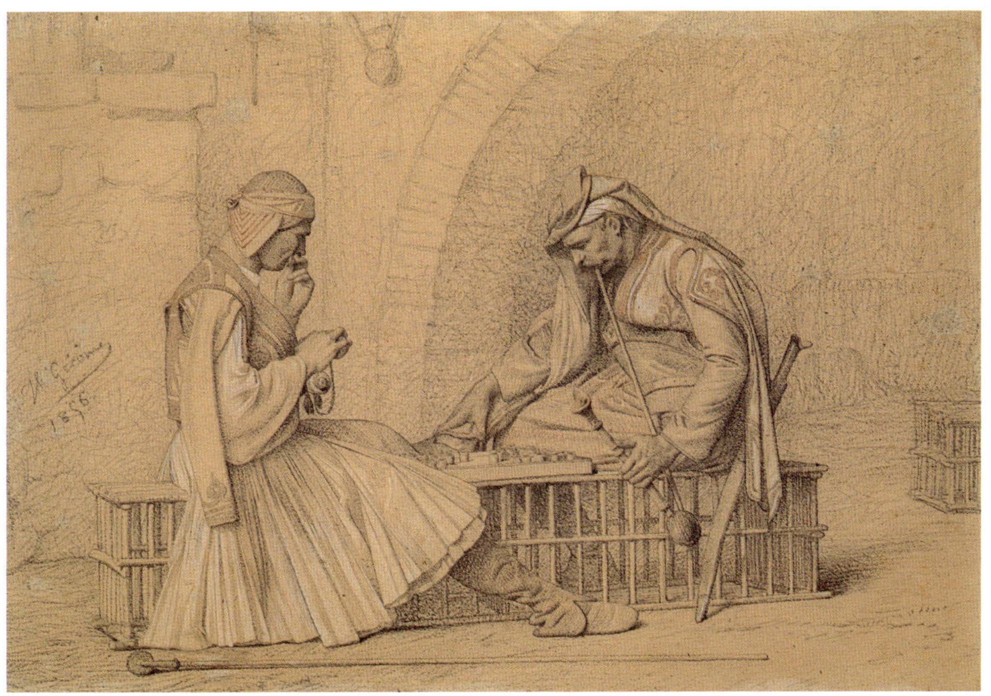

JEAN-LÉON GÉRÔME

French, 1824–1904
Two Soldiers Playing Checkers
1856
Chalk, pencil, and gouache
7¾ x 10¹³⁄₁₆ in. (19.6 x 27.5 cm)
Signed and dated left center:
J L Gérôme/1856
Acquired 1929 (Scott and
Fowles, New York)
1955.1656

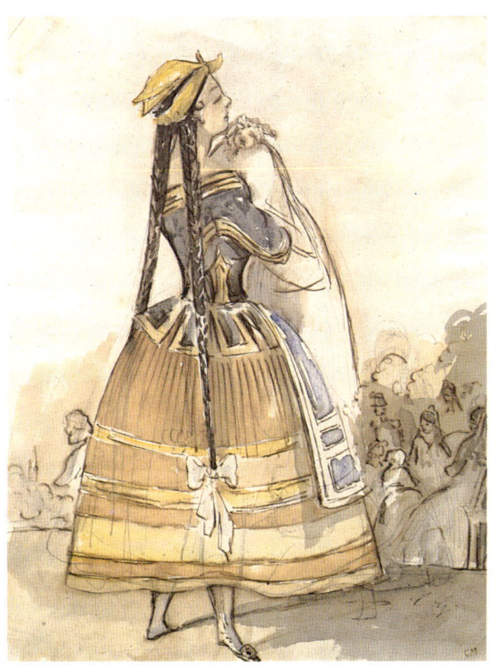

CONSTANTIN GUYS

French, 1802–1892
Amelia Masi
c. 1856
Ink and watercolor over pencil
11⅞ x 8⅞ in. (30.2 x 20.5 cm)
Signed lower right: *C. G.*;
inscribed upper right: *A Melia Masi*
Acquired 1916 (Knoedler, Paris)
1955.1926

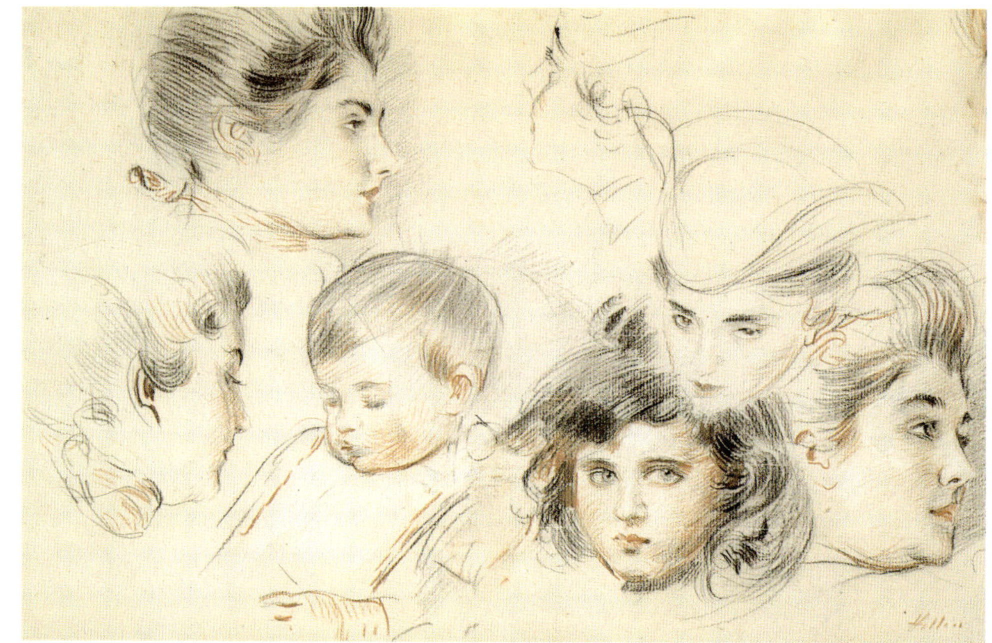

PAUL CÉSAR FRANÇOIS
HELLEU

French, 1859–1927
Studies of Heads
c. 1900
Chalk
10½ x 15¹¹⁄₁₆ in. (26.7 x 39.8 cm)
Signed lower right: *Helleu*
Acquired 1938 (Prouté, Paris)
1955.1669

EDOUARD MANET
French, 1832–1883
Woman in a Large Hat
1880
Watercolor
7 x 4¹⁵⁄₁₆ in. (17.7 x 12.5 cm)
Signed lower right: *E M*
Acquisition date unknown
1955.1916

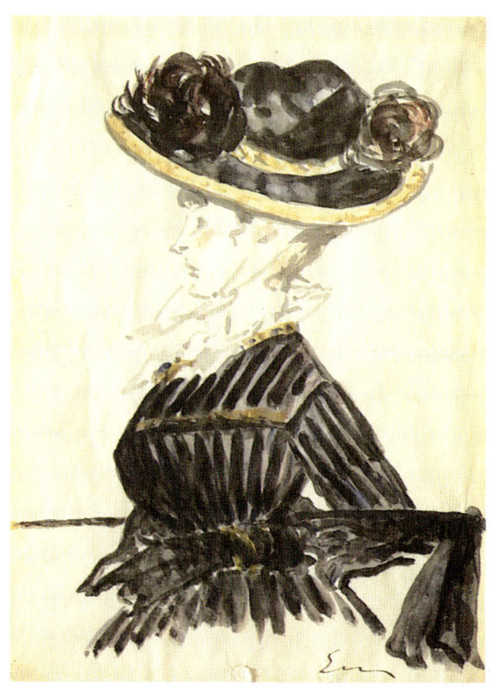

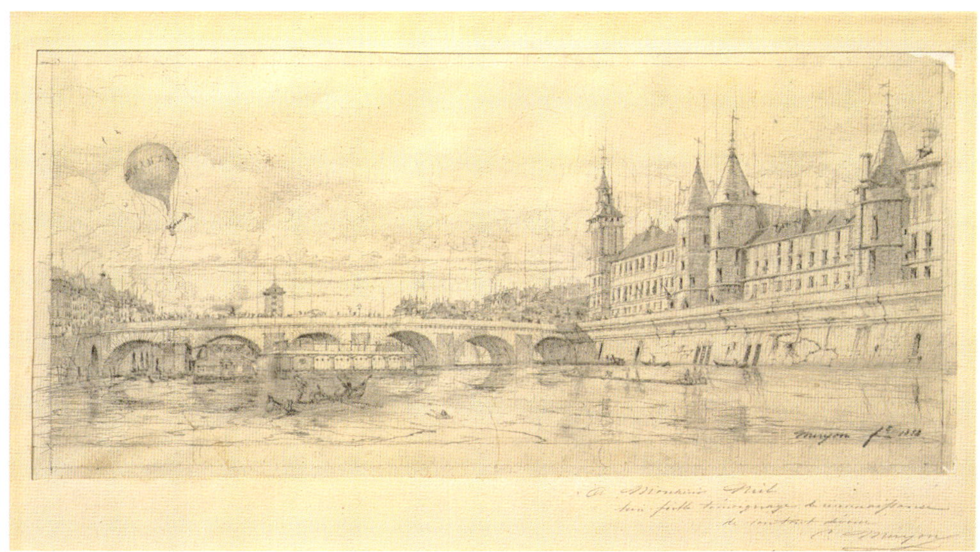

CHARLES MERYON

French, 1821–1868
Le Pont-au-Change, Paris
1852
Pencil
6³⁄₁₆ x 13⅛ in. (15.7 x 33.3 cm)
Signed and dated lower right:
Meryon ft 1852
Acquired 1917 (Knoedler,
New York)
1955.1856

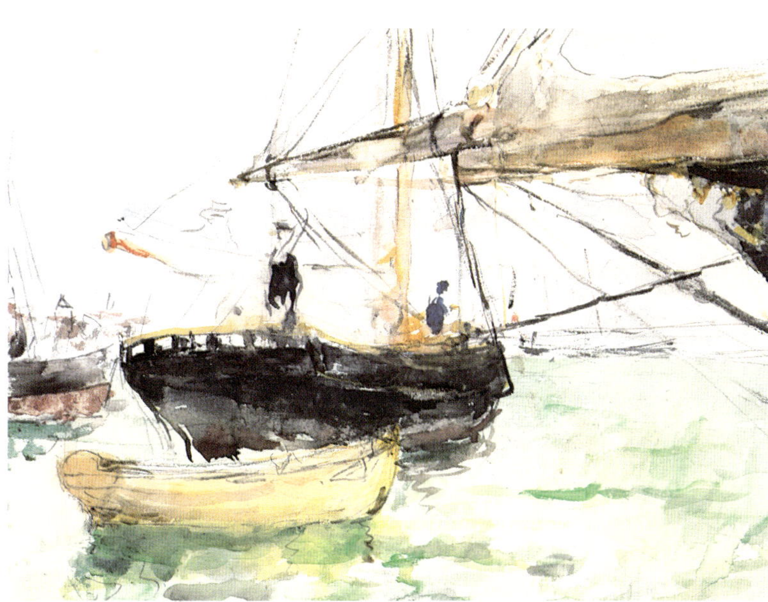

BERTHE MORISOT

French, 1841–1895
Harbor Scene
1875
Watercolor over pencil
8⅛ x 10½ in. (20.7 x 26.7 cm)
Signed lower left: *Berthe
Morisot*
Acquired 1939 (Carstairs,
New York)
1955.1964

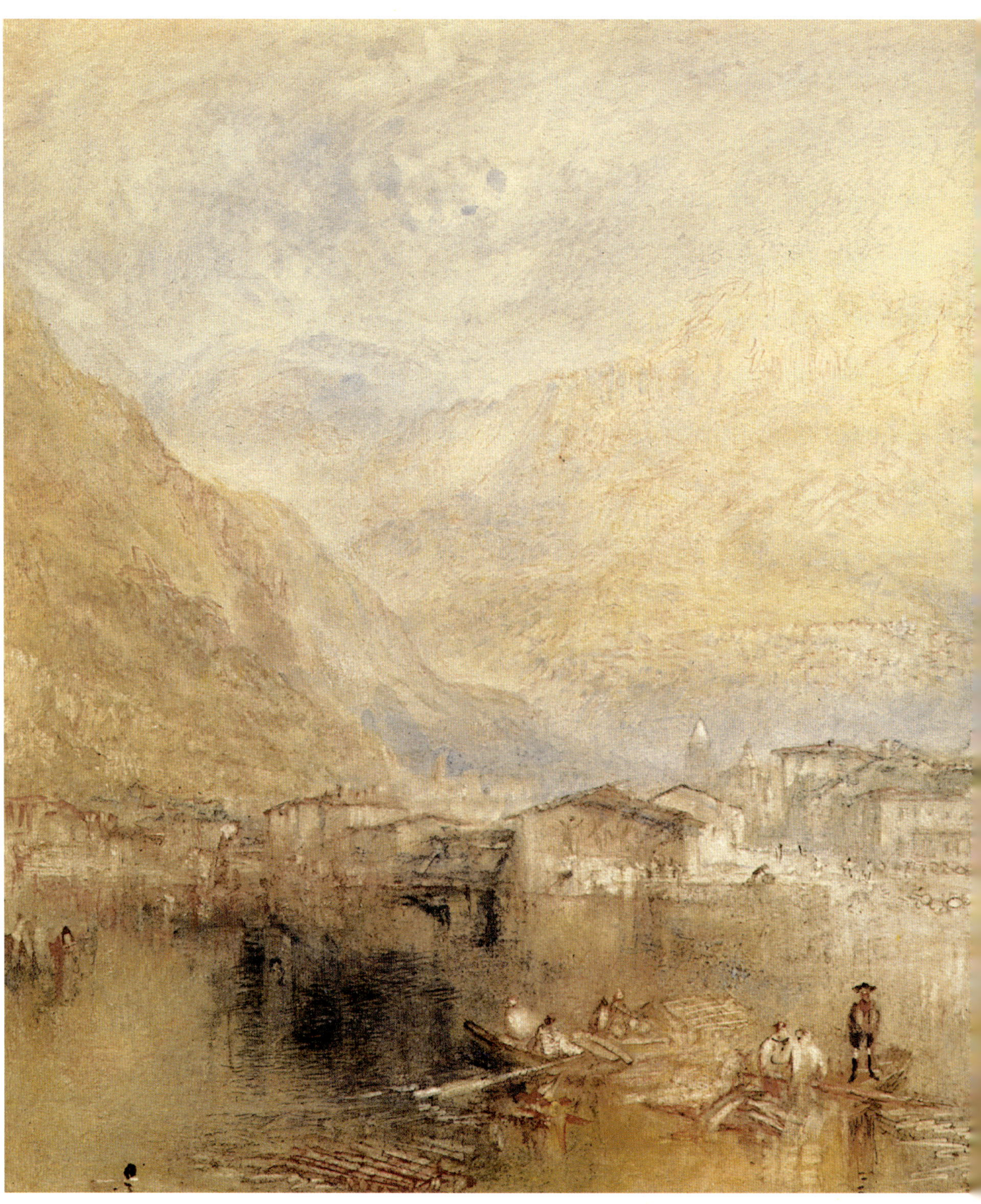

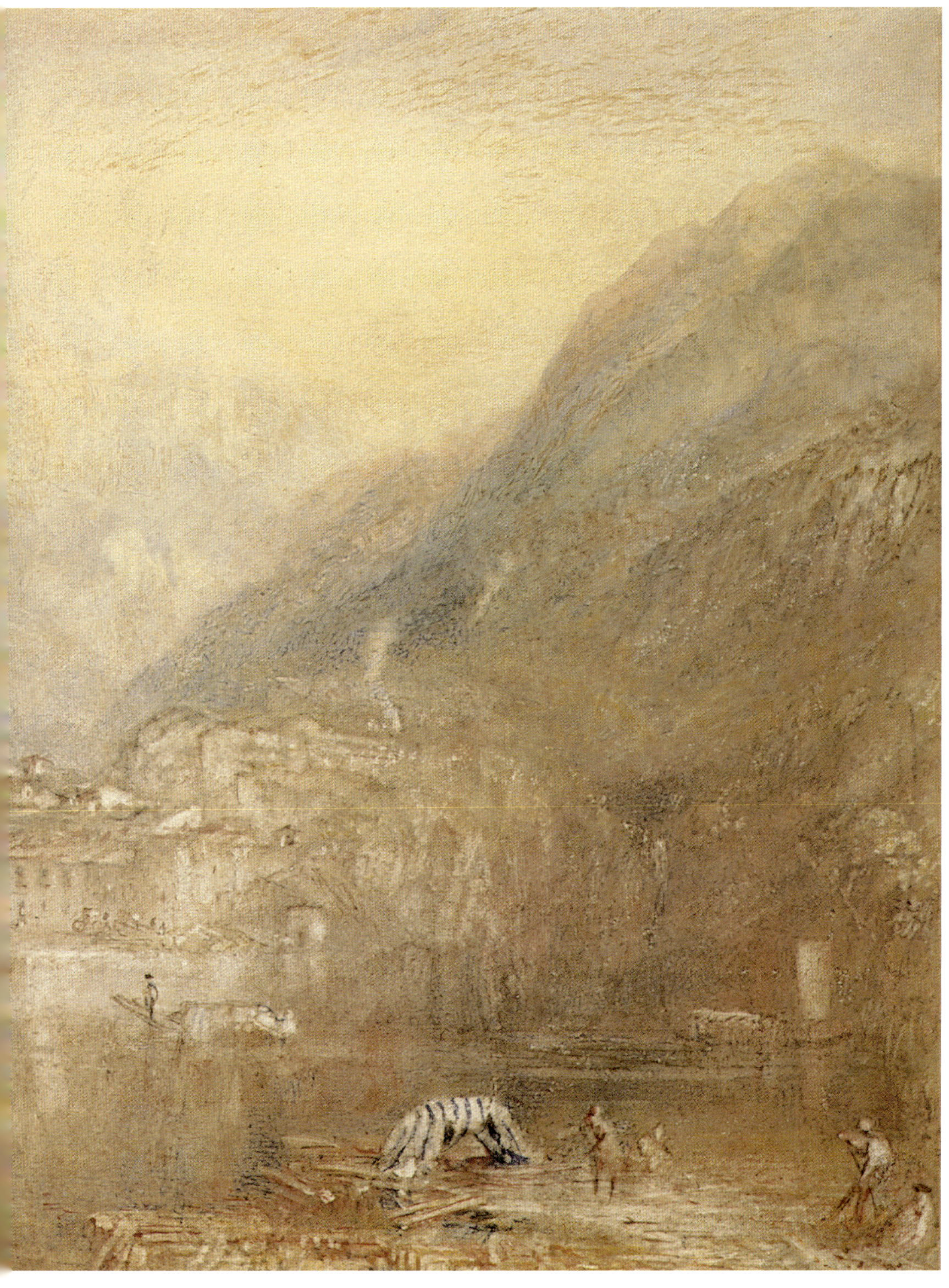

JOSEPH MALLORD
WILLIAM TURNER

British, 1775–1851
*Brunnen, from the Lake of
Lucerne*
1845
Watercolor and body color
11¹¹⁄₁₆ x 18¹³⁄₁₆ in. (29.7 x 47.8 cm)
Unsigned
Acquired 1941 (Scott and
Fowles, New York)
1955.1865

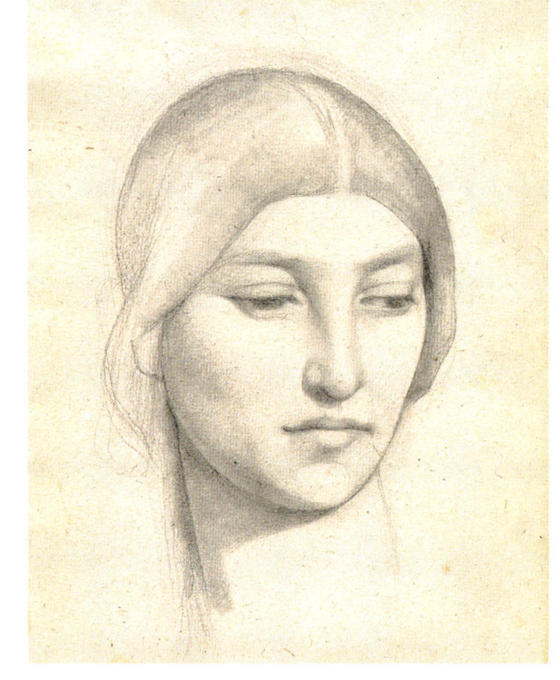

PIERRE PUVIS DE CHAVANNES

French, 1824–1898
Study of a Woman's Head
c. 1860–70
Pencil
6¾ x 5¼ in. (17.2 x 13.4 cm)
Unsigned
Acquired 1919 (Galerie Choiseul, Paris)
1955.1716

HENRI DE
TOULOUSE-LAUTREC

French, 1864–1901
At the Circus: "Chocolat"
1899
Chalk
10 x 14 in. (25.3 x 35.5 cm)
Signed with monogram
lower right:
Acquired 1942 (Carstairs,
New York)
1955.1428

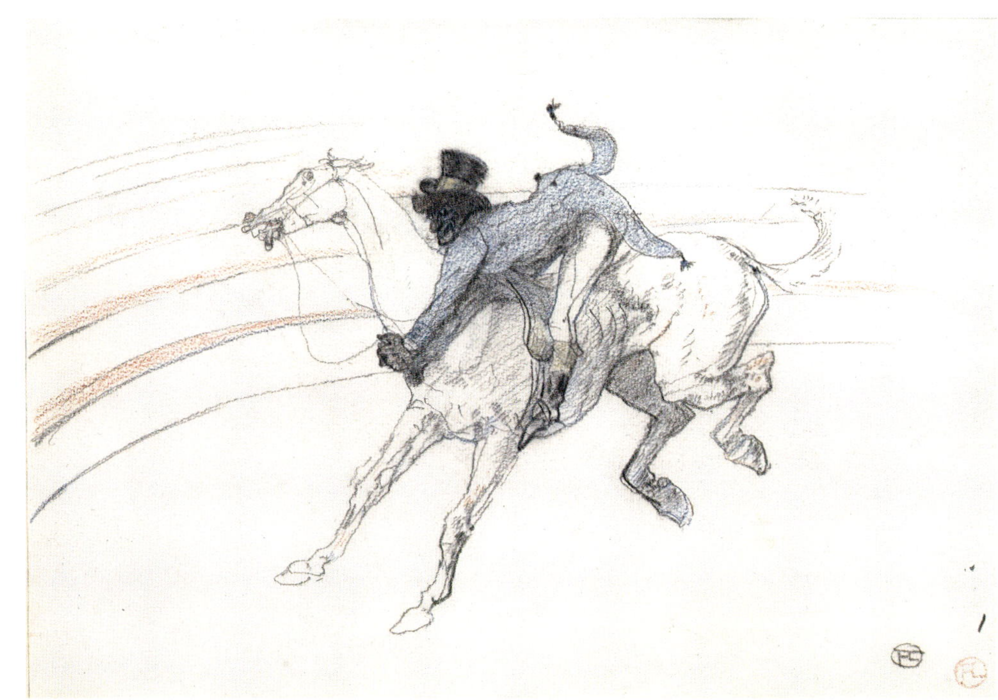

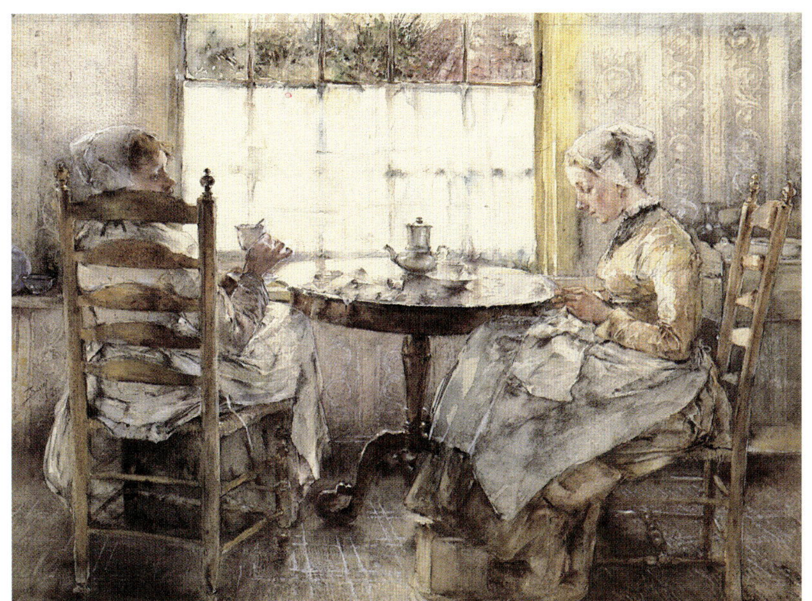

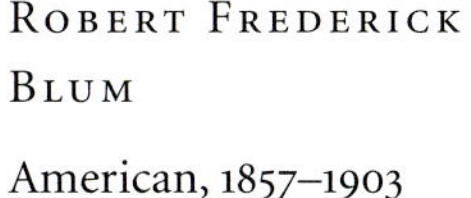

ROBERT FREDERICK
BLUM

American, 1857–1903
*Two Dutch Girls Having
Coffee*
1885
Watercolor and gouache over
pencil
12½ x 16⅟₁₆ in. (31.7 x 40.8 cm)
Signed and dated left center:
Blum/85
Acquisition date unknown
1955.1569

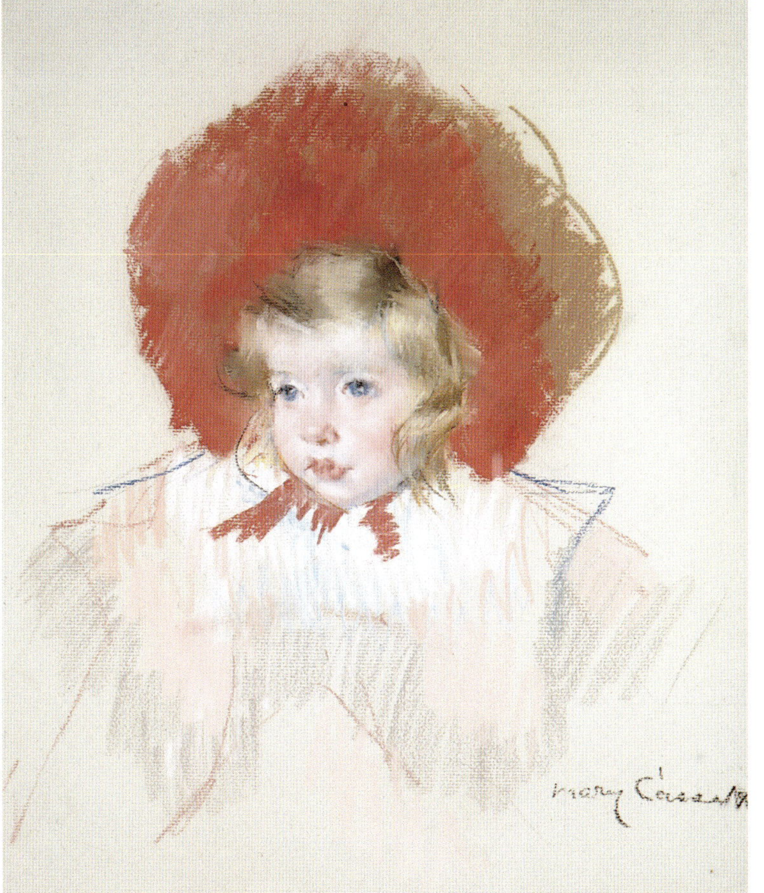

MARY CASSATT

American, 1844–1926
Child with Red Hat
c. 1904
Pastel
20¾ x 17⅛ in. (52.6 x 43.4 cm)
Signed lower right: *Mary
Cassatt*
Acquired 1935 (Knoedler,
Paris)
1955.674

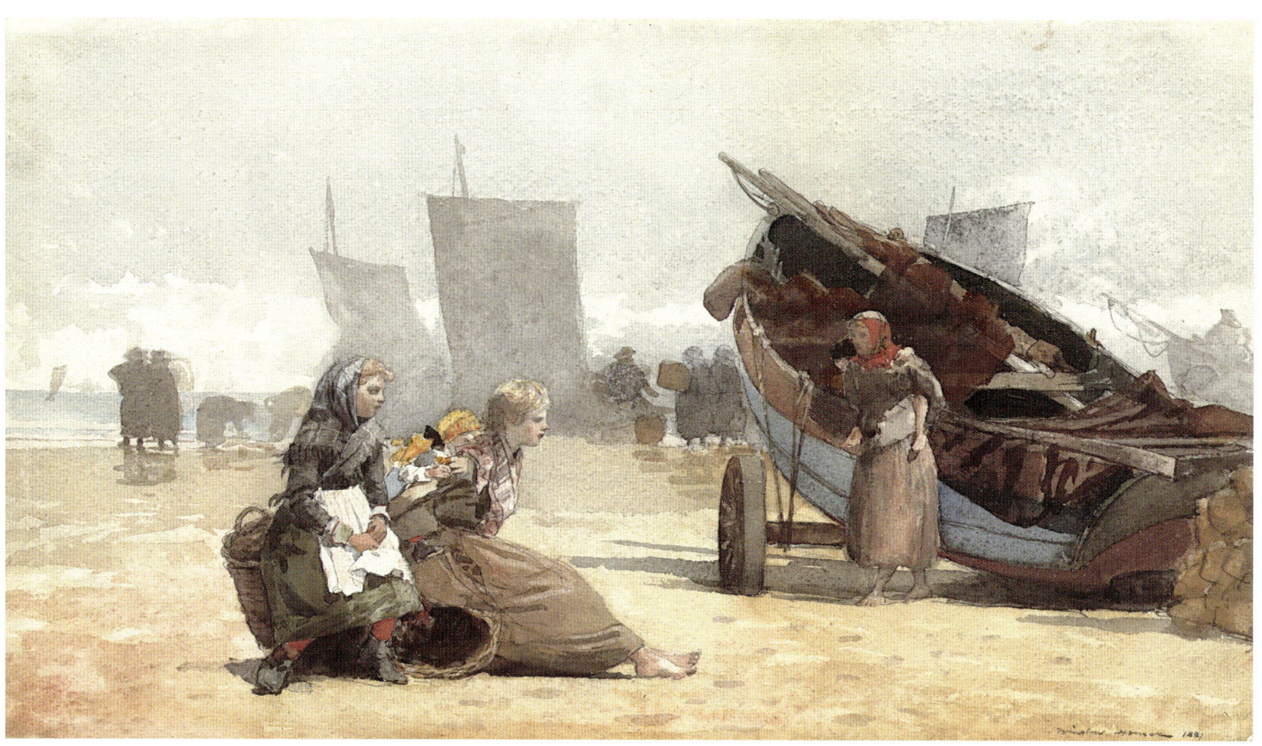

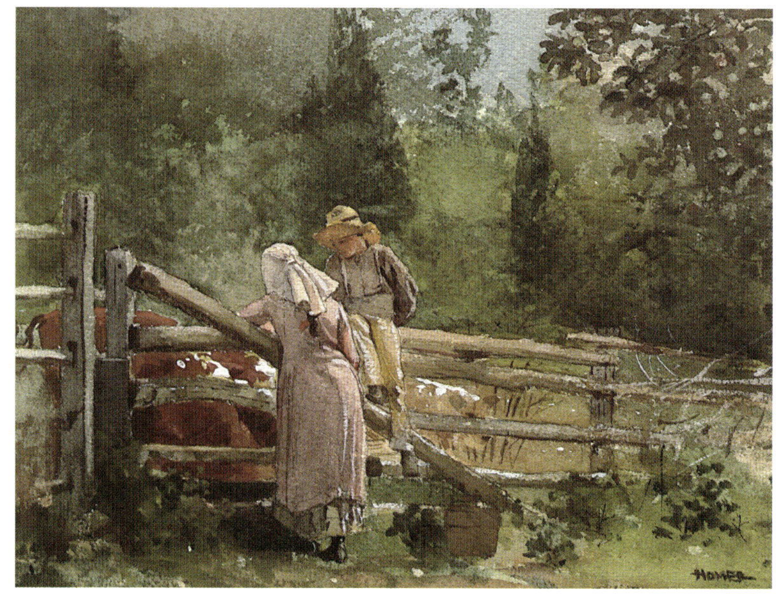

WINSLOW HOMER
American, 1836–1910
Beach Scene, Cullercoats (formerly *Beach
Scene, Tynemouth*)
1881
Watercolor and pencil
11½ x 19½ in. (29.1 x 49.6 cm)
Signed and dated lower right:
Winslow Homer 1881
Acquired 1924 (Knoedler, New York)
1955.1490

WINSLOW HOMER
American, 1836–1910
Feeding Time
c. 1878
Watercolor and gouache over pencil
8¾ x 11¼ in. (22.2 x 28.4 cm)
Signed lower right: *HOMER*
Acquired 1926 (Knoedler, New York)
1955.1493

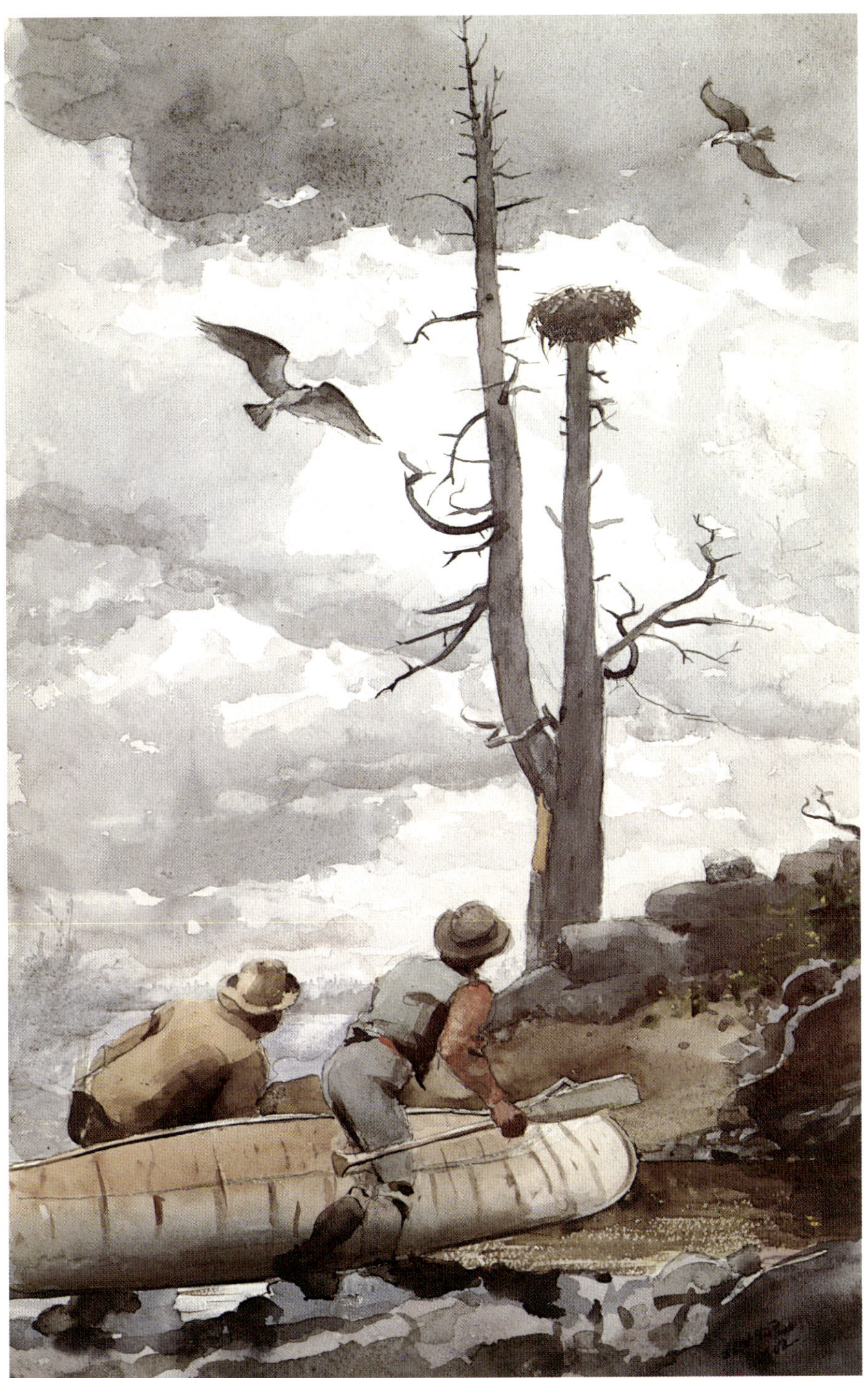

American 1836–1910
The Osprey's Nest
1902
Watercolor over pencil
21⁹⁄₁₆ x 13⁹⁄₁₆ in. (54.7 x 34.5 cm)
Signed and dated lower right:
HOMER/1902
Acquired 1917 (Knoedler,
New York)
1955.1502

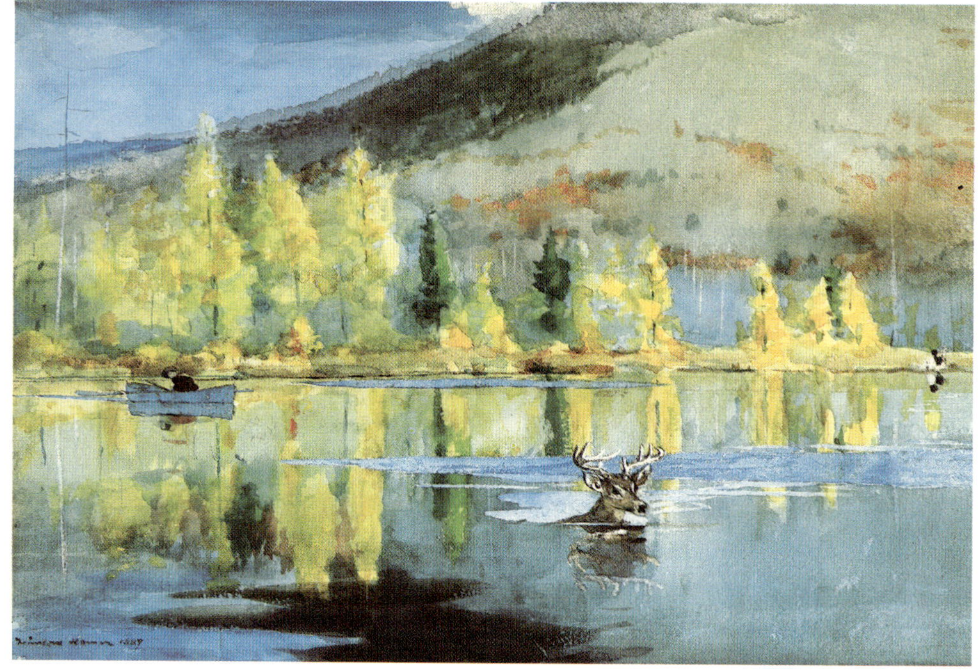

WINSLOW HOMER

American, 1836–1910
An October Day
1889
Watercolor
13⅞ x 19¾ in. (35.2 x 50.1 cm)
Signed and dated lower left:
Winslow Homer 1889
Acquired 1947 (Knoedler, New
York)
1955.770

JOHN LA FARGE

American, 1835–1910
Design for a Stained-Glass Window
1901
Watercolor over pencil on board
15¼ x 11¾ in. (38.8 x 29.9 cm)
Signed and dated lower left:
Jno LaFarge 1901.
Acquisition date unknown
1955.1679

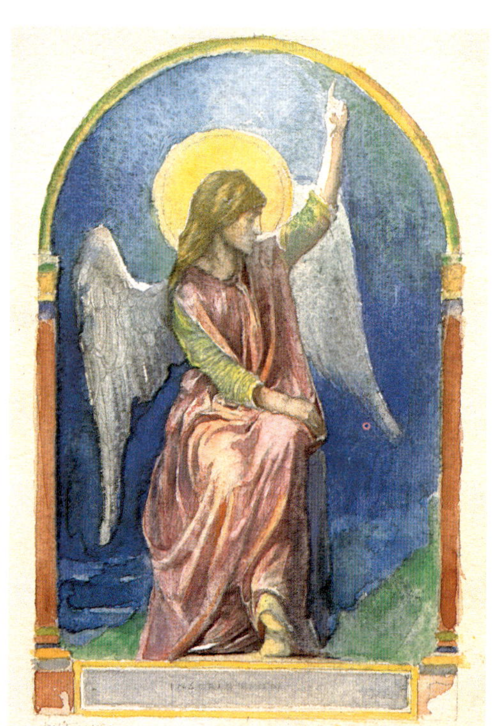

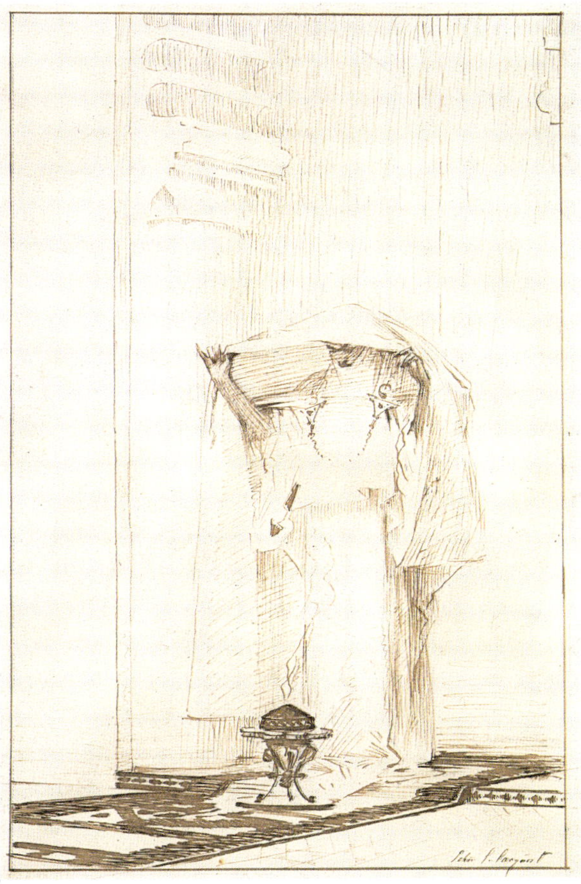

JOHN SINGER SARGENT

American, 1856–1925
Sketch after
"Fumée d'ambre gris"
1880
Ink
11⅜ x 7¹³⁄₁₆ in. (28.9 x 19.8 cm)
Signed lower right:
John S. Sargent
Acquired 1942 (Scott and
Fowles, New York)
1955.1737

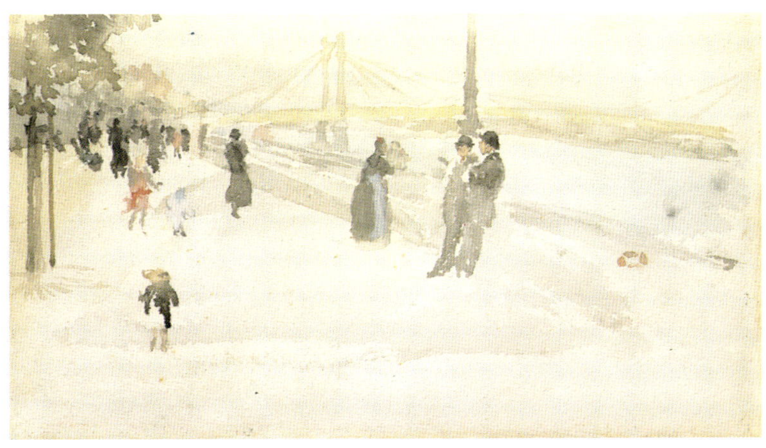

JAMES ABBOTT
MCNEILL WHISTLER

American, 1834–1903
Grey and Silver: Chelsea
Embankment
c. 1887
Watercolor
5 x 8½ in. (12.7 x 21.6 cm)
Signed with monogram mid-
dle right:
Formerly Alfred Corning
Clark Collection
1955.1533

LIST OF ARTISTS

Numbers indicate page(s) where artist's work appears.

Robert Frederick Blum *35*

Giovanni Boltraffio *16*

Jean Bourdichon *16*

Mary Cassatt *35*

Jules Chéret *25*

Gustave Courbet *25*

Honoré Daumier *25*

Hilaire Germain Edgar Degas *26, 27*

Eugène Delacroix *28*

Albrecht Dürer *17*

Jean-Honoré Fragonard *20*

Thomas Gainsborough *21*

Jean-Léon Gérôme *29*

Jean-Baptiste Greuze *20*

Constantin Guys *29*

Paul César François Helleu *30*

Winslow Homer *36, 37, 38*

John La Farge *38*

Edouard Manet *30*

Charles Meryon *31*

Berthe Morisot *31*

Pierre Paul Prud'hon *22*

Pierre Puvis de Chavannes *34*

Rembrandt Harmensz. van Rijn *19*

Peter Paul Rubens *18, 19*

John Singer Sargent *39*

Giovanni Battista Tiepolo *23*

Giovanni Domenico Tiepolo *23*

Henri de Toulouse-Lautrec *34*

Joseph Mallord William Turner *32–33*

Jean-Antoine Watteau *24*

James Abbott McNeill Whistler *39*